P9-DHI-353

THE HEAD BONE'S CONNECTED

TO THE NECK BONE

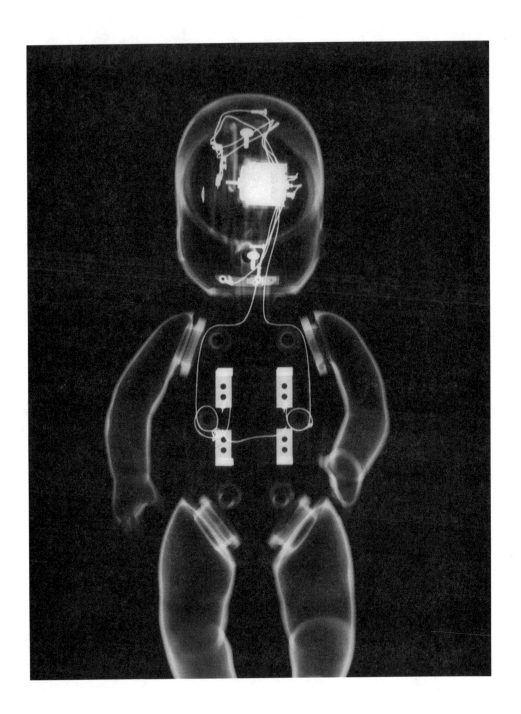

THE

HEAD

BONE'S

CONNECTED

THE WEIRD, WACKY, AND WONDERFUL X-RAY

TO THE

NECK BONE

CARLA KILLOUGH McCLAFFERTY

FARRAR, STRAUS AND GIROUX · NEW YORK

Distributed in Canada by Douglas & McIntyre Ltd.

Printed in the United States of America

Designed by Abby Kagan

First edition, 2001

10   9   8   7   6   5   4   3   2   1

Library of Congress Cataloging-in-Publication Data

McClafferty, Carla Killough, 1958–

The head bone's connected to the neck bone : the weird, wacky, and wonderful x-ray /
Carla Killough McClafferty.— 1st ed.

p. cm.

Includes bibliographical references and index.

ISBN 0-374-32908-7

1. Radiography, Medical—History—Juvenile literature.   2. X-rays—History—Juvenile
literature.   3. Radiography—History—Juvenile literature.   [1. X rays.   2. Radiography.]
I. Title.

RC78 .M315 2001

616.07'572'09—dc21

00-140218

This book was made possible, in part, by a grant from the Society of
Children's Book Writers and Illustrators.

Frontispiece: An X-ray depicting the internal mechanism of a drink-and-wet doll.

To the loves of my life—

my husband, Pat,

and my children, Ryan, Brittney,

and Corey, who is gone but not forgotten

CONTENTS

Prologue: A Glimpse at Yesterday   3

1. Discovery: No Humbug   5

2. The Skeleton Inside Me   20

3. Bullets and Bones   32

4. Trial and Error   45

5. Burned and Bald   52

6. Schemes and Dreams   77

7. Fake or Fact?   85

8. Secrets Revealed   95

9. The Industrious X-ray   110

10. What's Next?   117

Glossary   119

Selected Bibliography   123

Recommended Further Reading   125

Web Sites   127

Acknowledgments   129

Illustration Credits   131

Index   133

THE HEAD BONE'S CONNECTED

TO THE NECK BONE

PROLOGUE:
A GLIMPSE AT YESTERDAY

Life was different in 1895. The streets were crowded with horses instead of cars. The Wright brothers had not yet begun their experiments in flight; people took the train when they traveled across the country. The newly formed International Olympic Committee was planning to hold the first Olympic Games in over 1,500 years.

Many exciting things happened for the first time in 1895: an audience saw the first silent movie, men played the first professional football game in America, Guglielmo Marconi sent the first radio signal through the air, the first Kodak pocket camera was introduced, and the first flaked breakfast cereal was made.

The world of medicine was different, too. Doctors could not "see" inside their patients unless they performed surgery. If doctors suspected a patient had a broken bone, they pressed on the injured part, which could be very painful, then gave their best guess as to whether the bone was broken.

Things we take for granted in our lives today were not even imagined yet. There was no air conditioning, television, washing machines, vacuum cleaners, or frozen food.

Imagine living during that period of time. Now imagine you've just heard the news that a German scientist had discovered a way to see your bones right through your clothes and skin. The news was incredible. It was fantastic. It was creepy.

It was . . . true!

1 DISCOVERY: NO HUMBUG

The University of Würzburg
Würzburg, Germany
November 8, 1895

The room was dark. The laboratory in the Physical Institute at the university was deserted after the assistants had gone home. That is, all except for Dr. Wilhelm Conrad Roentgen, a physical scientist, who waited patiently to see the results of his experiment. In his personal laboratory, all was quiet except for the quick snapping sound the vacuum tube was making as an electric current ran through it.

Dr. Roentgen (in German his name is spelled Röntgen) was continuing his study of cathode rays, suspecting there was more to be learned than what other scientists had already found out. He was using a pear-shaped Crookes tube to produce the rays. A Crookes tube was made of glass, sized a little bigger than a man's hand. The tube would have most of the air pumped out of it, almost creating a vacuum. Inside were two electrical connections that allowed electricity to flow through the tube. The man who developed this contraption, William Crookes, and other scientists had demonstrated that when electricity flowed through the vacuum tube, electrons rushing from the negative connection (the cathode) to the positive

Dr. Wilhelm Conrad Roentgen as he looked at the time of his great discovery. Roentgen was not a medical doctor but a professor of physics. He earned a degree in mechanical engineering and a Ph.D. for his study of gases. But his school years were not always easy. When he was sixteen, he was expelled for refusing to identify a classmate who drew a not-so-flattering picture of his teacher.

One of the most important scientific discoveries of all time was made in this laboratory when Roentgen discovered X-rays. The room looks poorly equipped compared to today's sophisticated labs.

connection (the anode) caused invisible rays to be produced. The evidence of the presence of these rays, called cathode rays, was a brightly colored glow inside the glass tube. Scientists proved the rays could travel only a few centimeters through air.

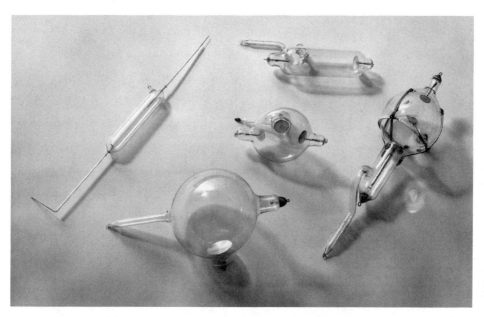

Some of the actual tubes used by Dr. Roentgen in 1895 and 1896 to produce X-rays. Although they are of different sizes, they all worked the same way and produced the same results. This type of tube came to be known as a cathode ray tube (CRT) and is used today in radar displays and televisions (the picture tube is a CRT).

Dr. Roentgen had covered his Crookes tube with black cardboard to see if the cathode rays could travel through the cardboard into the air. He watched in the darkness for any signs of the cathode rays, but saw none. The experiment was over. But wait—he saw something unusual out of the corner of his eye.

An eerie, yellowish-green glow appeared from the direction of his workbench, about a yard away. Since color blindness affected his ability to distinguish the color green, Dr. Roentgen passed the current through the tube again to be sure he really saw what he thought he saw. Yes, there it was again. He lit a match in the darkness to see where the glow was coming from. In the dim light, he saw a piece of paper coated with a fluorescent material called barium platinocyanide lying on his workbench.

In the darkness again, Dr. Roentgen watched as the glow from the paper flickered, changing from bright to dim, depending upon the strength of the electric current flowing through the Crookes tube. His source of electricity was an induction coil, but the amount of electricity that came from it fluctuated in strength. The stronger the current, the brighter the coated paper glowed; the weaker the electric current, the softer the glow of the paper.

He picked up the paper and walked farther from the tube. Even six feet away, the paper still had its strange glow. He knew the energized tube must be causing the paper to shine, but how? Cathode rays couldn't cause the glow because they couldn't travel that far outside the Crookes tube.

Roentgen placed a piece of writing paper between the tube and coated paper. The coated paper continued to glow as if the regular paper were not even there. Next, he placed a one-thousand-page book between the tube and coated paper. The paper was not as bright as before, but it still glowed.

He tested everything he could get his hands on: a double pack of playing cards, tinfoil, wood, rubber, glass, water, and aluminum. The paper glowed behind each object, brighter behind some than others. The only material that seemed to stop the paper's glow was lead. Roentgen wondered why the rays did not penetrate lead as he studied the shadow cast by the lead on the coated paper. Then he saw something no one had ever seen before.

Instead of seeing the shadow of his hand holding a piece of lead on the paper, Roentgen saw the image of a skeleton's bony hand. He couldn't believe his eyes. He was looking at the bones of his own fingers. It was incredible. It was impossible, wasn't it?

He was late for dinner that evening as he made his way up the stairs that connected his private lab to the apartment above. His wife and daughter knew he had something on his mind, since he ate in silence. During dinner, it occurred to him that he hadn't even taken notes on what he had seen, as he usually did when he worked. Had he actually seen the image of his own bones? How was it possible? Was it a freak accident? Could he reproduce what he had just seen?

He went back to his laboratory as soon as he had finished dinner. Roentgen checked the equipment to make sure it was set up as before. This time he took careful notes about every detail of the experiment.

The electric current surged through the tube. In the darkened room he saw it again: the image of his bones appeared on the coated paper. It wasn't a fluke. He could reproduce it. He knew this discovery was big, really big.

Wilhelm Conrad Roentgen, at fifty years of age, had discovered something previously unknown in the scientific world: a ray of energy so powerful it could penetrate most objects, including flesh and bones. He called his new discovery X-rays because x is the mathematical symbol for the unknown.

Dr. Roentgen knew he must find out everything he could about X-rays through careful experimentation. While he was conducting his research, he didn't tell anyone about his discovery. To his friend Theodor Boveri he said, "I have discovered something interesting but I do not know whether or not my observations are correct." In a letter to a friend on February 8, 1896, Dr.

Roentgen wrote, "I had not spoken to anyone about my work. To my wife I mentioned merely that I was doing something of which people, when they found out about it, would say, *"Der Röntgen ist wohl verrückt geworden"* ("Röntgen has probably gone crazy").

To get credit for making this discovery, he had to be the first to write a scientific paper about it and have it published. Other scientists besides himself were studying cathode rays. Had someone else discovered the X-rays, too? He must hurry to be the first to report it.

Dr. Roentgen wanted to work on his new discovery alone without the interference of his lab assistants. He sent them to do their work in one of the other laboratories in the Physical Institute building. He instructed the servants to bring his meals to him on a tray. Also, he had them bring a cot into the laboratory so that he could collapse onto it when exhaustion forced him to sleep. He later recalled, "I was not aware of anything else but the strange phenomenon in the laboratory. Was it a fact or an illusion? I was torn between doubt and hope, and did not want to have any other thoughts interfere with my experiments. I tried to exclude everything not pertinent to the laboratory work from my thinking." His intentions were clear to all who lived and worked at the university's Physical Institute: he did not want to be disturbed.

He was ready to begin his experiments. But first he needed a way to keep a permanent record of the objects he exposed to X-rays. Other scientists who had studied cathode rays before him found that they darkened photographic film, and so routinely used it in their experiments. Dr. Roentgen suspected X-rays would darken film, too. To test his theory, he placed a piece of platinum on a photographic plate and exposed it to X-rays. His hypothesis was correct. After the film was developed, the platinum showed up as a white spot on the black film. Now he had a way to preserve his work.

Most of his experiments were conducted in the dark to be able to see the effects of the X-rays. With each experiment, he covered all the windows in his laboratory with heavy blinds and curtains to make the room as dark as possible, then uncovered them when he was finished to write notes. This process wasted precious time. He needed a faster way to achieve darkness, and he knew just what he had to do: build a makeshift darkroom.

Roentgen built it big enough to hold his six-foot-one-inch-tall body, plus the few inches of hair that stood straight up from his head. The wooden box was seven feet high and four feet square. He cut a door out of one side and built a shelf inside the box. The box was big enough for him to go inside, shut the door, sit on a stool, and have some elbow room for conducting his experiments.

He covered the outside of the huge box with sheets of zinc. Next, he cut a circle out of one side eighteen inches across and covered it with a thin layer of aluminum. He chose these two metals because he found by testing various metals that zinc stopped most of the X-rays, while aluminum allowed X-rays to pass through it almost as if it wasn't there. This way, Roentgen knew the only X-rays coming into the box were passing through the aluminum circle, not through the sides of the box. As an added precaution, to keep the photographic plates from getting any exposure from the rays until he was ready to use them, he added an extra lead plate to the outside of the zinc box on the side where the tube would be located.

Dr. Roentgen didn't know at the time that overexposure to X-rays could be dangerous to your health, but the zinc-covered box he built for a darkroom ended up protecting him from the harmful rays. It may even have saved his life.

The huge box was positioned with the Crookes tube on the outside, just five inches from the aluminum circle. As usual, Dr. Roentgen built his own instruments to test the X-rays, and placed them inside the box.

He took X-ray photographs of various things: a closed wooden box filled with metal weights, a compass, and a section of zinc that had been pieced together to show the differences of each strip and the welds that held them together. He also took an X-ray of his double-barreled shotgun. One X-ray of the door in his laboratory surprised him. The film showed that few of the X-rays went through the door—because it had been painted with lead paint.

After he had exposed the photographic plates to the X-rays, they had to be developed. Dr. Roentgen found a photographer he could trust and swore the man to secrecy about the strange, shadowy images he would see on the film he developed. Roentgen was the only person in the world that knew about the existence of X-rays while he conducted his experiments. For a lot of people, this would have been a hard secret to keep.

A little more than six weeks after his discovery, he was ready for the final experiment before he

This X-ray image of a compass was one of the first films taken by Dr. Roentgen. The lines and letters show up because they were painted with lead paint. Dr. Roentgen documented his X-ray images on specially prepared glass plates—very different from the flexible film used today.

announced the news to the world. To accomplish this test, he enlisted the help of his beloved wife, Bertha.

He invited Bertha into his laboratory on December 22, 1895. Roentgen asked her to place her hand on a photographic plate underneath the funny-looking glass tube. He instructed her to keep her hand completely still for fifteen minutes. Bertha did as he asked.

Roentgen could hardly wait until the film was developed. He expected Bertha to be as excited as he was about what she was going to see.

Bertha looked at the X-ray of her own hand. A chill raced down her spine. She was terrified as she gazed upon her own ghostly image. Her wedding ring looked as if it were floating around the bones of her own skeleton. She worried that seeing her own bones was an omen that her life would be cut short.

It wasn't. Bertha lived to the ripe old age of eighty.

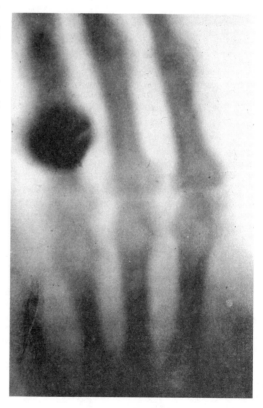

The world's most famous X-ray: the hand of Bertha Roentgen, Dr. Roentgen's wife. Copies of this film were sent all over the world. It is often referred to as the first X-ray. It was not the first X-ray, but it was the first one taken of another person. Roentgen exposed Bertha's hand to the X-rays for fifteen minutes to get this image. Today, an X-ray of a hand takes 1/30 of one second.

After the final test of Bertha's hand, Dr. Roentgen was ready to publish his discovery. Just seven weeks after he discovered X-rays, his experiments and scientific paper were finished. The paper, titled "On a New Kind of Ray," described all he had learned. Wilhelm and Bertha Roentgen walked together to mail the paper to the Würzburg Physical-Medical Society to be published in their journal. As he dropped it in the box, Roentgen told his wife, "Now the devil will have to be paid." He seemed to foresee the uproar his discovery would cause after his paper was published on December 28, 1895.

The first page of Dr. Roentgen's report describing his discovery, handwritten in German. In English, the title means "On a New Kind of Ray (Preliminary Communication)."

Dr. Roentgen proved the basic properties of X-rays during his experiments, but it would be years before the scientific world understood that X-rays are only one type of energy that travels in waves called electromagnetic radiation. Radio waves, radar waves, microwaves, and visible light are some other types of electromagnetic radiation. Light is the only one we can see with our eyes.

If you think of these forms of energy as waves, then the main difference between each one is the wavelength—how close together or far apart each wave is to the next one. For example, radio waves are far apart, maybe the length of a football field, while X-ray waves are very close together, around the length of a single molecule.

The closer the waves are to each other, the more powerful they are. It's just like ocean waves rushing to the beach: if the waves come in fast, one right behind the other, they have more power than if there was one wave and five minutes later there was another. Fast, frequent waves rolling onto the beach can knock you off your feet, but usually one wave by itself won't.

The same thing is true for all electromagnetic radiation. It is the waves that rush in fast, one right behind the other like X-rays, that are powerful enough to penetrate solid objects. That is the reason X-rays can go through your body and visible light waves cannot—X-rays have a shorter wavelength, which means the waves of energy are closer together.

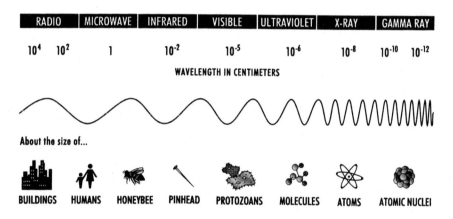

| RADIO | MICROWAVE | INFRARED | VISIBLE | ULTRAVIOLET | X-RAY | GAMMA RAY |

10^4 10^2 1 10^{-2} 10^{-5} 10^{-6} 10^{-8} 10^{-10} 10^{-12}

WAVELENGTH IN CENTIMETERS

About the size of...

BUILDINGS   HUMANS   HONEYBEE   PINHEAD   PROTOZOANS   MOLECULES   ATOMS   ATOMIC NUCLEI

Although different types of electromagnetic radiation have different wavelengths, they all have one thing in common: each kind travels at the same speed—the speed of light, which is about 669,600,000 miles per hour, or 186,000 miles per second. That is even faster than kids leaving school on the last day before summer vacation!

The first announcement to the public about Dr. Roentgen's discovery of X-rays appeared in a newspaper in Vienna, Austria. On January 5, 1896, the Vienna *Presse* published the news under the heading "A Sensational Discovery."

THE LIGHT THAT NEVER WAS.

A Photographic Discovery Which Seems Almost Uncanny.

Special to The Post-Dispatch.

NEW YORK, Jan. 7.—A cablegram to the Sun from London says: The noise of war's alarms should not detract attention from the marvelous triumph of science which is reported from Vienna. It is announced that Prof. Routgen of the Wurzburg University has discovered a light which, for the purpose of photography, will penetrate wood, flesh and most other organic substances. The Professor has succeeded in photographing metal weights which were in a closed wooden case; also a man's hand, which shows only the bones, the flesh being invisible.

Newspaper reports of the discovery of X-rays, like this one from the *St. Louis Post-Dispatch*, were printed all over the world. Notice that Dr. Roentgen's name is misspelled, as it was in newspapers everywhere, and that it says a man's hand was photographed by the new rays. No one knew at this time that the hand belonged to Roentgen's wife, Bertha.

It was so unbelievable that when the London *Standard* reported it, the newspaper ended its article by assuring readers that "there is no joke or humbug in the matter. It is a serious discovery by a serious German Professor."

News of the discovery of X-rays by Dr. Wilhelm Conrad Roentgen spread throughout the world like a juicy piece of gossip. The shy German professor was suddenly catapulted to fame. Dr. Roentgen had gone from being an unknown scientist working hard in a laboratory to being the man who had discovered the incredible X-ray. He was the subject of many newspaper and magazine articles. Reporters from all over the world wanted to interview him, and people everywhere wanted to talk to him. And he didn't like it. As he took his daily walks, so many people spoke to the suddenly famous scientist that he grumbled he was about to wear out a new hat from greeting people. All he wanted was to go back to his laboratory and do more research on X-rays. He complained in a letter to a friend, "For exactly four full weeks I have been unable to make a single experiment! Other people could work, but not I. You have no idea how upset things were here."

Invitations to give lectures about his discovery poured in from everywhere. But he didn't want to speak about X-rays, he wanted to learn more about them. He refused all requests but one. He gave a lecture to the Physical Medical Society in his hometown of Würzburg, Germany, on January 23, 1896. It was the only lecture he would ever give about X-rays.

On the evening of the lecture, scientists, doctors, military and local authorities, and as many students as could squeeze into the room gathered to hear their own professor speak about his discovery. Wild applause, feet stamping, and a standing ovation broke out across the room when Dr. Roentgen entered. A bit embarrassed by the reception given him, he began to speak about his discovery. At the conclusion of the lecture, Dr. Roentgen asked Albert von Kölliker to allow him to take an X-ray photograph of his hand. The elderly anatomy professor was delighted to sit still while the X-ray was taken. The crowd tingled with excitement as they were given the extraordinary privilege of witnessing the discoverer of X-rays take an X-ray—although there really wasn't much to see. When the developed film was shown to the crowd, the entire lecture hall roared with approval and excitement. Von Kölliker was so thrilled he led the audience in three cheers for Dr. Roentgen and suggested the rays be called "Roentgen rays" from that moment on. Copies of the X-ray of von Kölliker's hand were later sold to the public.

However, Dr. Roentgen did not want X-rays to be called by his name. He believed that a natural phenomenon like X-rays should not be attributed to a person. Throughout his lifetime, he corrected anyone who used the term "Roentgen rays" in his presence and told them they were X-rays.

As soon as he could, Dr. Roentgen continued his research on X-rays and eventually published two more reports on the subject.

Kaiser Wilhelm II, the German Emperor, was delighted that a German had made this wonderful discovery. He insisted that a statue of Dr. Roentgen be erected in honor of the event. But Dr. Roentgen did not want a statue made in his image. Being modest about his accomplishments, he was embarrassed to be honored in such a way. Besides that, he didn't want to waste his time posing for a sculptor. But when the Emperor wanted something, you couldn't stop him.

Statue of Dr. Roentgen, placed on a bridge in Berlin, Germany, at the insistence of Kaiser Wilhelm II. Roentgen didn't like the statue because he thought the artist made the X-ray tube look like an insect sprayer. He complained that the public would see his statue holding the ridiculous-looking device on the bridge forever. He was wrong. Near the end of World War II, metals for making war supplies became scarce in Germany. The government took the sculpture from the bridge and melted it down.

Through the years, Dr. Roentgen was honored in many different ways, but the most important was in 1901. He was given the first-ever Nobel Prize in Physics, which included a diploma, a gold medal, and a cash prize of 150,800 Swedish kronor.

Aside from the prize, Dr. Roentgen never accepted any money for his discovery of X-rays. When a German electric company asked him to work with them to further develop X-rays, Dr. Roentgen replied, "According to the good tradition of German university professors, I am of the opinion that their discoveries and inventions belong to humanity and that they should not in any way be hampered by patents, licenses, contracts, nor should they be controlled by any one group."

In 1900, at the request of the German government, Dr. Roentgen became the director of the physics department at the university in Munich. He worked there until his retirement in 1920, a year after Bertha died.

Even after his official retirement, two laboratory rooms were set aside at the university for the distinguished professor's private use. Until his death on February 10, 1923, about six weeks before his seventy-eighth birthday, Dr. Roentgen walked to his laboratory regularly to continue his work.

In his will, Dr. Roentgen gave the University of Würzburg his diplomas, addresses, and medals, and left instructions that the cash he received for winning the Nobel Prize be used for scientific research. Except for a few personal belongings, he gave everything else to charity. After his death, as in life, Dr. Roentgen wanted to retain his privacy. He left instructions that his personal and scientific papers be burned at his death, without being read. The world will never know what went up in flames as the notes and papers of this brilliant scientist turned to ashes.

2 THE SKELETON INSIDE ME

The news of the discovery of X-rays swept around the world. Some people who heard the news thought it must be a joke. The idea of seeing through skin was so incredible that one of Roentgen's friends wrote, "I could not help thinking that I was reading a fairy tale, though the name of the author and his sound proofs soon relieved me of any such delusion."

An article in *The New York Times* on January 16, 1896, reported:

Men of science in this city are awaiting with the utmost impatience the arrival of European technical journals, which will give the full particulars of Prof. Routgen's [*sic*] great discovery. . . . Prof. Routgen of Würzburg University has recently discovered a light which, for purposes of photography, will penetrate wood, paper, flesh, and nearly all other organic substances. Thus, the bones of the human frame can be photographed in relief without the flesh which covers them. . . .

The fascination with X-rays was so strong that within a few weeks Dr. Roentgen's paper "On a New Kind of Ray" had been translated into all the major languages in the world. By the end of 1896, several books and a thousand papers on the subject of X-rays had been published.

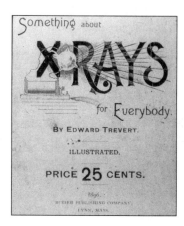

Front cover of one of the first books published in English on the subject of X-rays (1896).

Journals and newspapers rushed to publish details of Dr. Roentgen's apparatus and copies of the X-ray of Bertha Roentgen's hand. This was possible only because Dr. Roentgen refused to obtain a patent on his X-ray machine or a copyright on the X-ray he had taken. If he had, no one else could have built a machine like his or used his X-ray films without paying him. He would have made a fortune, but he chose to allow his discovery to be used without any limitations on it. Following his lead, the X-ray tube makers did not patent their tubes, either, so they could be used legally everywhere.

When people saw bony images from X-rays for the first time, they were amazed, they were disgusted, they were fascinated, they were horrified . . . and they wanted to see more.

On February 15, 1896, *The New York Times* reported: "Probably never before has the entire scientific world been simultaneously aroused to such a pitch of excitement as that caused by the recent remarkable discovery of Prof. Roentgen of Wuerzburg. . . ." The subject so fascinated the public that newspapers and magazines were in a hurry to publish something about X-rays, *anything* about X-rays, whether it was true or not. They could write whatever they wanted on the subject because no one knew anything about it. Most of the scientific facts they printed were true, but not all. And some of their ideas about how X-rays could be used were impossible.

It was a fact that X-rays could pass through clothing as if it weren't there. People were fascinated by that truth and began to have ridiculous ideas about how this could be used. It didn't help when articles were published that described X-rays as "modern photography" and the "wonder camera of the Würzburg professor." This gave the public the impression that an X-ray was just like taking a photograph with a regular camera, except the finished picture showed the bones of people instead of their outer appearance. This thought captured the imagination of many writers and artists who created poems, jokes, and cartoons about it. In 1896, this poem appeared in the journal *Photography*:

X-actly So!

The Roentgen Rays, the Roentgen Rays,
What is this craze?
The town's ablaze
With the new phase
Of X-ray's ways.

I'm full of daze,
Shock and amaze;
For nowadays
I hear they'll gaze
Thro' cloak and gown—and even stays,
These naughty, naughty Roentgen Rays.

Cartoons like these misled people
into thinking X-rays were just like
photographs, except that they
showed the bones of people.

The idea that X-rays could see through clothing confused the public. They didn't understand that if the rays went through people's clothing, they would also go through their body. Many people worried that Peeping Toms could somehow use X-rays to see through the clothing of women right down to their naked skin. One shop owner in London saw his chance to cash in on this fear. He offered his clients "X-ray-proof underclothing." The only way underwear could be X-ray-proof would be if it was made from lead. OUCH!

Advertisements in magazines for "X-ray opera glasses" caused concern for the modesty of those on the American opera stage. Assemblyman Reed, a member of the New Jersey state legislature, introduced a bill to his state assembly that would have made it illegal to use "X-ray opera glasses" in the theater.

The public didn't understand that X-rays were produced only with certain equipment connected to an electrical source. And even then, an X-ray film must be used to see the effects of the rays.

X-ray images of any kind were a fascination to all who saw them. A bootmaker in London placed two films in the window of his shop that caught the eye of people passing by. One X-ray showed a foot with misshapen bones caused by wearing a shoe that didn't fit properly. The other showed the sole of a boot with all the nails and brads in it. The bootmaker hoped his customers would assume that the boot on the X-ray caused the foot damage, and that the boot was made at another store.

Some were not so excited about the use of the X-ray "ghost pictures." The London journal *The Electrician* wrote: "We cannot agree with the newspapers in regarding this discovery as a revolution in photography;

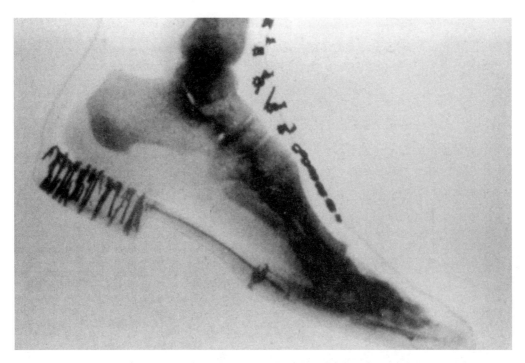

This rare X-ray of a foot inside a boot was taken in March 1896 by Dr. Francis H. Williams of Boston. In the
early days, many X-rays were taken of hands, but few were taken of feet. Notice the nails in the heel and
the metal grommets that held the shoelaces. The X-ray exposure time for this film was twenty minutes.
Today, an X-ray of a foot would be exposed for 1/20 of one second.

there are very few persons who would care to sit for a portrait which would
show only the bones and the rings on the fingers."

X-ray images scared many people who were seeing their own bones for
the first time. A newspaper editor had an X-ray taken of his skull, but when
he saw it, he "absolutely refused to show the picture to anybody but scientists. . . . He has not closed an eye since he saw his own death head."

But more often X-rays inspired creativity. Anyone from businessmen to farm boys who were curious set out to build his own apparatus. One man successfully built an X-ray tube out of the glass chimney of a kerosene lamp. He even produced an X-ray of a mouse with it.

Since everything was made by hand using any materials that could be found, every X-ray machine and X-ray studio was different. Some people opened studios in their homes, using their couch as an X-ray table. Other X-ray rooms had a special table built or used hospital stretchers.

Scientists were interested in X-rays, too, of course. Thomas Edison, the famous American inventor, worked to pro-

WONDERFUL NEW RAY SEES THROUGH HAND!

X-Ray Studio...

110 East Twenty-Sixty Street,

....New York City.

X-ray studios sprang up all over. Anyone who learned how to build X-ray equipment and produce a film could go into business taking X-rays of people.

duce X-rays as soon as he heard the news of the discovery. It was reported in *Electrical World* that "Edison himself

Wolfram Fuchs's X-ray laboratory opened for business in February 1896 in Chicago. He was an electrical engineer with a reputation for taking excellent X-ray films. Mr. Fuchs was one of the first to show gallstones on an X-ray. Notice the different X-ray tubes, the induction coil (front right), and the framed images. Mr. Fuchs died of radiation injuries in 1907.

has been having a severe attack of Röntgen mania. . . . Mr. Edison and his staff worked through seventy hours without intermission, a hand organ being employed during the latter hours to assist in keeping the force awake." Their hard work produced a working X-ray machine.

By February 8, 1896, *The New York Times* reported that Mr. Edison would "demonstrate the penetrating powers of the new light by an experiment in photographing a man's brain." The idea of seeing an image of a living brain thrilled reporters so much that twenty of them waited outside Edison's laboratory for three weeks to be among the first to report it.

But news from the Edison lab was slow in coming. On February 12, 1896, the *Times* reported that "Mr. Edison will first try to obtain an impression of the small bones of the inner ear by placing a negative plate . . . in the mouth and directing the Roentgen rays on the ear from the outside. Then he will probably try to get a photographic view of the skull from above by placing the electric bulb above it, and the negative plate in the mouth."

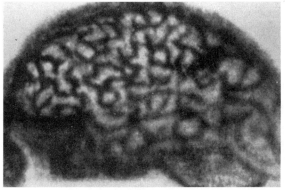

Does this look like an X-ray of a brain to you? It is actually a pan of cat guts arranged in the shape of a brain. The image was taken by Hilbert L. Falk of New Orleans and published in *The Electrical Engineer* in April 1896. When readers expressed their doubts, a team of investigators went to Mr. Falk's office. After watching his "method" of taking an X-ray, a spokesman for the team concluded that "in regard to the so-called X-ray pictures of Mr. H. L. Falk, I do not hesitate to say that they are spurious, and that Mr. Falk is a perfect humbug."

Day after day went by without the announcement of a successful brain X-ray. It seemed as if Mr. Edison was not going to produce the picture after all. One by one the reporters left their positions outside the Orange, New Jersey, laboratory. Thomas Edison did not succeed in producing an X-ray of the brain because all that can be seen on an X-ray film of the head is the skull bones, not brain tissue. It would be years before an X-ray of the brain itself could be obtained.

Thomas Edison did succeed in inventing a new tool for seeing X-ray images called the fluoroscope. This was a handheld device that looked like a megaphone. The patient was placed between the X-ray tube and the fluoroscope. The operator looked through the small end to see the X-ray image displayed on the screen at the wide end. The screen at the wide end was coated with a substance called calcium tungstate. After studying 1,800 different substances, Edison chose this one because it was highly fluorescent when X-rays hit it.

An early fluoroscope (1896) being used by one of the many women who worked with X-rays. The X-ray tube is just out of view in front of the woman's left hand.

The first public display of Thomas Edison's fluoroscope took place in May 1896 at the Electric Light Association Exposition in New York City. Edison's fluoroscope provided the public with a way to see X-rays in action. Edison built a special fluoroscope for the occasion with a screen that was larger than normal. It was big enough to see a person's entire arm at once.

Almost two thousand people lined up to

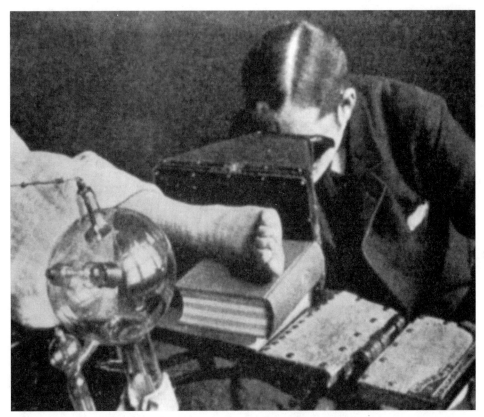

A doctor looking through a fluoroscope screen at a patient's ankle in 1910. Notice he isn't using an X-ray film, only the fluoroscope. This means that when the machine was turned off, the image was gone and there was no permanent picture. Also notice that the bare tube is only a few inches from the patient and doctor—not a good idea, since this practice later proved to be dangerous.

see their own bones. One hundred people at a time filled the large room where the demonstration was held. A hush fell over the noisy crowd as they were led into the darkness of the exhibit room. The walls and windows were covered with black drapes to keep light out so the audience's eyes would be accustomed to the darkness and better able to see the effects of the X-rays. The only lights that could be seen were two small red ones that dimly lit the way, and the glow of the fluoroscope screen.

The line of people twisted back and forth as if at an amusement park. Signs were posted that suggested a coin or a key be placed in a glove so it could be seen with the X-rays. The crowd crept closer and closer to the glowing screen. When a visitor's turn arrived at last, she was told in a serious, quiet voice to put her hand behind the screen with her palm turned toward her face and her fingers pressed together. Suddenly, she saw the image of her own bones only inches away.

Most people were delighted at the sight, but there were a few who were afraid to look at the terrible ghostly image once their turn came. A few took a quick peek, then made the sign of the cross and hurried out.

Mr. Edison's assistants kept a close watch on the equipment as the crowd went through. If any in the crowd had deformities or injuries that showed up on the X-ray fluoroscope, Edison's assistants referred them for a medical ex-

Almost two thousand people lined up to look at their own bones through the fluoroscope during Thomas Edison's demonstration in New York in May 1896. On the right, one of Edison's assistants is checking the strength of the X-ray tube by looking at his hand through a small handheld fluoroscope.

amination to Dr. William J. Morton. Dr. Morton, a well-known New York doctor, was the first physician to write an English-language book about X-rays.

The public was fascinated by the X-ray images they saw, and many were willing to buy one. The American Technical Book Company offered X-rays for sale that were "all life size and handsomely mounted." There were various choices, including:

A life-size view of a nine-week-old infant, or an adult torso shown from chin to pelvis. Each sold for $2.00.

A set of adult knee films, taken for a court case involving a trolley car accident. One knee was normal, the other showed a fracture. 75 cents.

A view of a child's elbow joint with a fracture and dislocation. 60 cents.

A film of a normal kidney and one containing a kidney stone. 50 cents.

An X-ray of human teeth, showing roots and fillings. 50 cents.

Only two years after the discovery, it became fashionable in New York for ladies to have an X-ray portrait made of themselves. Dr. William Morton was quoted in *The New York Times* in May 1898, saying, "A good many women have their hands taken just for fun, perhaps for a family souvenir." One woman was so pleased with her X-ray that she hung a copy of it in her window.

3 BULLETS AND BONES

Some pioneers in the field of studying X-rays immediately realized the possibilities for medical use after they saw the film of Bertha Roentgen's hand. On January 7, 1896, a German newspaper, the *Frankfurter Zeitung*, reported:

> At the present time, we wish only to call attention to the importance this discovery would have in the diagnosis of diseases and injuries of bones, if the process can be developed technically so that not only the human hand can be photographed but that details of other bones may be shown without the flesh. The surgeon then could determine the extent of a complicated bone fracture without the manual examination which is so painful to the patient; he could find the position of a foreign body, such as a bullet or piece of shell, much more easily than has been possible heretofore and without any painful examinations with a probe.

Not only did these suggested X-ray uses happen, but many more uses would be found as professionals of all types, including doctors, scientists, photographers, engineers, and even bookkeepers, took up working with X-rays. They were truly pioneers. They had no one to teach them, no book to read about the subject, no instructions to follow. There was no one they could question, because no one knew anything about these mysterious rays. They had to figure it out as they went along.

In the early days, even the major hospitals of the world considered X-rays to be experimental and not very important. No one was sure if the use of X-rays in some doctors' practices would be a lasting part of their patients' treatment or a passing fad. Because of this uncertainty, the location of the X-ray room was not a priority for hospitals. They placed the room in any nook or cranny they could find. Sometimes it would be a closetlike room in the basement or under a staircase, maybe even a section of a waiting room that had been partitioned off.

The X-ray pioneers didn't care how cramped or stuffy the rooms were. They were just happy to get the chance to experiment. Every available space in their tiny room was filled with extra glass X-ray tubes. They didn't have electric lights and wall sockets in every room as we have today. The electricity came from a coil in the room that was connected to the X-ray tube. The wires that connected them sometimes ran around the room, and up the wall, and hung from the gaslight fixtures on the ceiling.

When these pint-sized X-ray rooms were ready for the first patient, they were not only cluttered but sometimes looked frightening. Dr. Mihran Kassabian, considered to be an expert on the subject of X-rays, wrote a textbook published in 1907 titled *Röntgen Rays and Electro-Therapeutics*. In it he described how the X-ray operator should prepare the patient for an examination: "Those that are timid should be previously instructed to ignore noises, flashes, etc., necessarily occurring during the examination."

Occasionally, having an X-ray taken could be an electrifying experience. In his book Dr. Kassabian told about a case when "the machine emitted great sparks and once or twice gave the patient a shock."

Disregarding the difficulties, many all over the world eagerly began using X-rays. Pioneers everywhere were doing the same type of work at the same time, yet there was no common name for their field of study. Different people called it different things, such as Roentgenology, radiology, skiagraphy, actinography, diagraphy, scotography, fluoroscopy, and kryptography. Among other names, the film that was produced was sometimes called a radiograph.

X-rays took the guesswork out of finding foreign objects in the body. Before X-rays were possible, anyone who had been shot with a gun was in for a lot of pain when the doctor arrived. There was no way to know where the bullet ended up once it entered the body. To find the bullet, the doctor put a probe in at the entrance wound and dug around, this way and that way. After the discovery of X-rays, a film could be taken of the patient with a gunshot wound that showed the exact location of the bullet or bullets without using the probe.

FACING PAGE: This man's hand is full of shotgun pellets from an accidental shooting. The exact location of each pellet can be seen on the X-ray image, eliminating the need for a lot of painful probing. This film was made in February 1896 by Michael Pupin of Columbia University in New York City. It was the first time a fluorescent screen was used on top of the film to allow a shorter exposure time. Screens are still used today for the same reason.

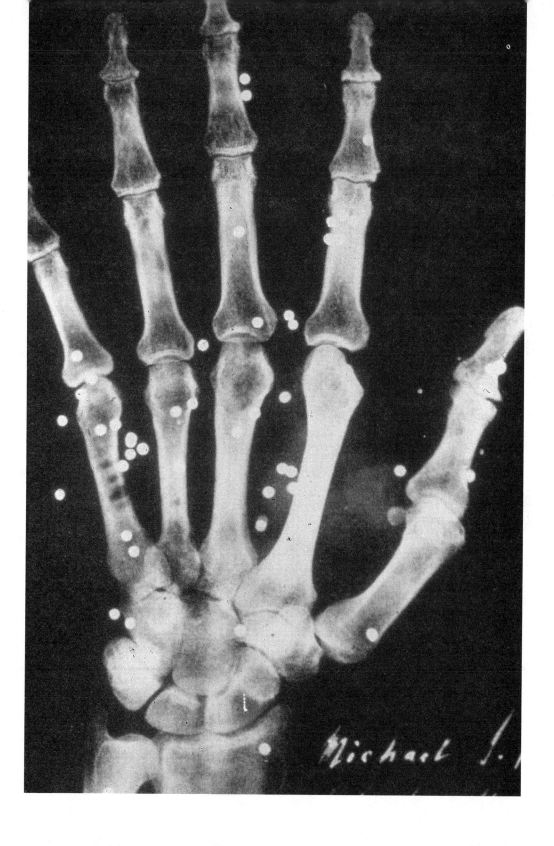

Michael J.

The British Journal of Photography reported how X-rays made a difference in the treatment of a gunshot wound to the hand:

> The surgeon . . . knew there were pellets imbedded in the hand, but they did not know that there were no fewer than twenty-four shots. Under ordinary circumstances, the surgeon might have removed twenty-two, and the two remaining might have caused serious trouble afterwards. On the other hand, he might have removed twenty-four, and still have been "fishing" for more. Owing to the radiograph taken of the hand, he knew the exact number of pieces of lead he had to extract.

Other foreign objects besides bullets could be located with X-rays. One man in Germany had constant pain from an old scar on his hand caused by the explosion of a laboratory glass. He had an X-ray taken of his hand that showed there was still a piece of glass imbedded there. A surgeon was then able to remove it, and his pain was gone as soon as the glass was.

Have your parents ever told you not to put anything except food in your mouth because you might swallow it? One ten-year-old boy in 1896 probably wished he had listened to his folks after the nail he had in his mouth went down his throat. Dr. R. Poech spoke about his case to a Society of Physicians: "He immediately had difficulty in breathing and was very much frightened. A physician was called who introduced a coin catcher and a probe into the oesophagus, but when he found no resistance he thought that the nail had gone down into the stomach. The physician advised him to eat large quantities of mashed potatoes." A few days later, the boy started having feverish coughing fits lasting for up to an hour and a half at a time.

X-rays showed that instead of swallowing the nail, the boy had actually breathed it into his lungs! During one coughing fit, the nail could be seen on the fluoroscope moving "up and down for a distance of from 4 to 5 cm." Surgery was performed, and thanks to the X-rays, the surgeon knew exactly where the nail would be.

Even dentists couldn't resist using X-rays when they saw how well they demonstrated the anatomy of teeth, including the roots hidden in the gums. They began using X-rays to diagnose some of their patients' dental problems. Cavities were visible on film, as well as impacted teeth, which are teeth wedged and stuck below the surface of the gum line and unable to come out naturally.

At first it seemed X-rays were useful only for seeing bone fractures, foreign objects, and teeth, since the body's organs, veins, and arteries had not yet been visualized. However, E. Hascheck and O. T. Lindenthal of Vienna, Austria, were about to change all that.

In January 1896, they wondered if the veins could be seen under the skin if they were filled with a substance that would show up on X-rays. They reasoned that since both chalk and bones contain calcium, perhaps chalk would show up on X-rays as bones do. To test their theory, they made a liquid concoction that contained a lot of chalk. They wanted to inject this

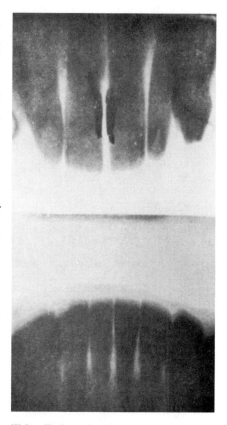

Walter König, a physicist in Frankfurt, Germany, made this early dental X-ray on February 1, 1896. The exposure took nine minutes. Although the film's quality isn't good enough to diagnose cavities, you can see the space between the patient's two upper front teeth and the metal fillings, possibly gold, along the middle edges.

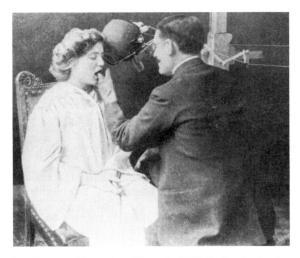

A patient receiving a dental X-ray in 1910. Notice the dentist holding the film in her mouth with his hand during the X-ray. This practice eventually damaged the fingers of many dentists.

mixture into the veins of a person to see if it would work. Since none of them wanted to inject their own bodies with the mixture, they looked around for someone who wouldn't mind. Finding no volunteers who were still using their body parts, they ultimately had to use the hand of a corpse. A local doctor supplied them with the necessary part taken from the body of an old woman.

They injected the mixture into the hand and took an X-ray. The experiment was a success. The film clearly showed the veins in the hand. The experimenters reasoned that other organs of the body might also be visualized on film, such as the stomach, intestines, gallbladder, and brain. They were correct, and solutions safe enough to be given to living patients were developed over the years that allowed all of these body parts to be visualized with X-rays.

Even while incredible advances were being made with X-rays in those early days, there were some doctors who refused to have anything to do with them. They considered X-rays to be strange and almost magical. Dr. Lewis Gregory Cole of New York City was in medical school when X-rays were discovered. His interest in surgery was replaced by his fascination with using X-rays to diagnose his patients' problems. First he used them to study broken bones. Next, when he took an X-ray of the spine, he noticed that the faint shadow of the kidneys could be seen as well. He thought, since kidneys could be visualized on film, then maybe X-rays could be used to diagnose kidney stones. Over time, he proved that kidney stones could be diagnosed using X-rays. From that point on, he routinely looked for any additional information he could find from all his X-rays.

In January 1896, this hand was amputated from the corpse of an old woman and injected with a mixture that showed up on film. It was the first X-ray that showed the veins of the body. A copper wire was wrapped around the hand's index finger to show differences between bone, metal, and the chalky solution they injected. Injecting a solution into blood vessels so they show up on X-rays is still performed today. This method is even used to study the arteries of a beating heart.

Dr. Cole noticed that when he took X-rays to diagnose broken ribs, he sometimes saw shadows in the patient's lungs he suspected to be lesions caused by tuberculosis. Could it be possible to diagnose tuberculosis with X-rays? To find out, he needed to take X-rays of the lungs of people who were known to have died of tuberculosis. For this, he needed specimens to study. He asked an old friend who was a pathologist—and therefore had access to cadavers (dead bodies)—to let him have some infected lungs. The friend refused, saying, "Young man, there is nothing to this X-ray diagnosis. It is nothing more or less than black art, and any one who attempts to use it is a charlatan."

Dr. Cole got his specimens elsewhere and proved that X-rays could be used to diagnose tuberculosis. And the friend who wouldn't let him have the infected lungs eventually died of tuberculosis.

Dr. Cole was not the only one who faced resistance by those who disapproved of X-rays. Dr. Heber Robarts, who in 1897 established the first publication in America devoted to the study of X-rays, *The American X-Ray Journal*, later recalled how some physicians felt in the early years. "I was looked upon by some doctors as an adventurer unworthy of consideration, and by others as flaunting defiance at their practice and intelligence. The x-ray was denounced by some leading men in our profession—by teachers in surgery, diagnosticians, pathologists and practitioners. It was regarded by them as foolery, spectacular only, and fit for the quack's armamentarium."

But no amount of discouragement would stop the early trailblazers as they looked for more ways to use X-rays. And it didn't take long for another—unexpected—use to be found.

Dr. Leopold Freund of Vienna, Austria, read about a man whose hair

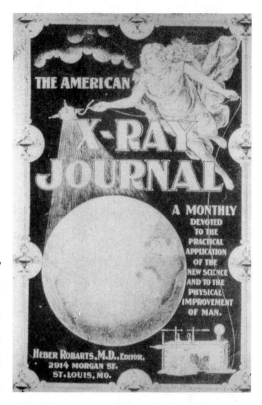

The May 1897 cover of *The American X-Ray Journal*, the first publication of its kind in the United States. It was begun in St. Louis, Missouri, by Dr. Heber Robarts to share information about what was happening all around the world in the X-ray profession.

fell out after working with X-rays. He wondered if X-rays could be used to *treat* his patients' problems as well as diagnose them. He soon got a chance to test his theory.

In November 1896, J. M. Eder, a professor at the Physiological Institute of the University of Vienna, allowed Dr. Freund to use his X-ray machine. Professor Eder later described a patient of Dr. Freund's in this way:

One of his first subjects was a little girl who was so badly disfigured by a tremendous fur-like hairy pigmented birth mark that her parents insisted upon having the hair removed. Freund irradiated his little patient daily for two hours for a period of ten days. One day, while I was working in my laboratory, the door was opened suddenly and without being announced he excitedly burst into the room pulling the little girl behind him and shouting, "Herr Director, the hair has come out." He was right. There was a small circular bald spot on the girl's neck as the result of the irradiation.

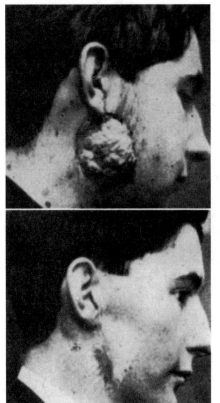

TOP: **A young man with cancer in 1901.**

BOTTOM: **Eleven months later, after**

successful X-ray therapy.

Dr. Freund began a new branch of medicine when he successfully treated that four-year-old. It would become known as radiation therapy.

Doctors supposed that if X-rays could get rid of a hairy birthmark, maybe it could get rid of the thick, dark birthmarks, called strawberry marks, that many babies are born with. It worked; the therapy caused them to disappear.

Next, doctors recommended radiation therapy to treat skin cancer. The use of X-rays in cancer treatment was successful. The before-and-after pictures that were published of these patients were so amazing that it seemed radiation therapy was a miracle cure. In fact, radiation therapy works so well in treating some cancers that it is still in use today.

Since skin problems of all types responded positively to X-ray therapy, it seemed these treatments were the answer to almost every problem. Doctors began prescribing X-ray therapy for patients who had conditions as varied as asthma, eczema, whooping cough, acne, ringworm, shoulder pain, depression, and any problems a woman might have with her reproductive organs. More than one hundred

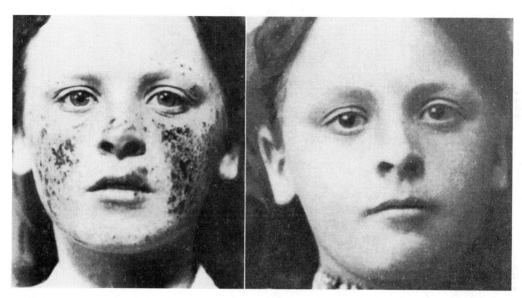

This twelve-year-old girl had a skin problem called eczema. The photos show her before and after X-ray treatments. Even as late as 1957, one million people per year were receiving radiation therapy for non-life-threatening conditions.

different diseases or conditions, most of them not life-threatening, were treated with X-ray therapy over the years. But these treatments were not as safe as originally thought.

At the time, the radiation therapy Dr. Freund used on his first patient caused painful sores on the little girl's back, but she recovered and lived a normal life. However, photographs of the same patient taken when she was seventy-four years old show that long-lasting damage was done.

Other children who were treated with X-rays for non-life-threatening skin problems later had skin damage as a result of therapy. In some cases, plastic surgery was needed to repair the sores and warts left behind.

In 1905, this X-ray therapy room at London Hospital was set up to treat ringworm of the scalp. Three patients could be successfully treated at once. In spite of its name, ringworm has nothing to do with worms—this contagious skin infection is caused by a fungus. X-ray therapy is no longer a treatment for it; today, it is treated with medication by mouth and ointment.

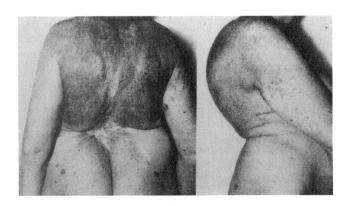

Dr. Freund's patient seventy years after X-ray treatment removed a birthmark from her back. She had some lasting effects from the rays: scarring, skin growths, and a humpback.

4 TRIAL AND ERROR

Only two months after their discovery was announced to the world, X-rays were already being used in a court of law. On March 20, 1896, *The British Journal of Photography* reported the case of Miss Gladys Ffolliott, a comedy actress in England who hurt her foot when she fell down the stairs as she left the stage to change her dress. A month later she was still unable to work. To prove her injury was real, her doctor sent her to have both her feet X-rayed. The X-ray of the injured foot clearly showed a fracture when compared to her uninjured foot. As a result, there was no doubt about her claim. An article in the *Literary Digest* said: "Those medical men who are accustomed to dealing with 'accident claims'—and such claims are now very numerous—will perceive how great a service the new photography may render to truth and right in difficult and doubtful cases."

The same year, Colonel C. F. Lacombe of the Mountain Electric Company in Denver, Colorado, set up an X-ray machine and offered to take X-rays for free as a public service. Crowds of people came to him, not just because they were curious to see what their bones looked like, but, as Walter

Wasson, a local doctor, later put it, because they "were certain that their physicians were wrong, and wanted x-ray photographs to prove it." Colonel Lacombe subsequently made it a rule that no one would be X-rayed unless their doctor was with them. It's possible that most of these people were hoping to find enough evidence of malpractice to sue their doctors. And it wasn't long before it happened.

The very first case in the United States that used X-rays as evidence began on December 2, 1896, in Denver, Colorado. James Smith, a law student, had fallen off a ladder and injured his left thigh. His doctor, W. W. Grant, a well-known surgeon who was the first to perform an appendectomy in the United States, did not think it was broken and told him to exercise the leg.

The pain in James's leg was so severe that he knew his treatment would require more than just exercise. His injury also resulted in his left leg's being shorter than it had been before. When he heard that X-rays could show bone injuries, he had one taken of his leg. The film showed a break in his femur, the thigh bone. He sued Dr. Grant for malpractice, claiming he misdiagnosed his fracture, and sought $10,000 in damages.

Otto Glasser, in his account of the court case of James Smith, wrote that X-rays were taken of Smith's leg by Mr. H. H. Buckwalter. He was considered an expert in the field of X-rays "because he had been making shadowgraphs for the past eight months." The best film he took of his leg used an exposure of one hour and twenty minutes. (Today, radiologic technologists would expose a similar X-ray for a fraction of one second.)

When the trial began, the courtroom was packed with people who wanted to see if X-rays would be used. The judge, Owen LeFevre, wasn't sure if he should allow them as evidence in his court, since they had not been introduced before in any courtroom in America. He contacted judges in other parts of the country for their advice. One of them answered that he would not permit it "because there is no proof that such a thing is possible. It is like offering the photograph of a ghost when there is no proof that there is any such thing as a ghost."

Dr. Grant's lawyers argued that the "x-ray photographs" should not be allowed as evidence because the witnesses had not seen the actual broken bone but only a photograph that suggested the bone was broken.

The case made history in the American justice system the next day when Judge LeFevre ruled,

SCIENCE AND LAW MEASURE SWORDS

An artist's rendering of the people involved in the court case of James Smith against Dr. Grant, from the December 3, 1896, issue of the Denver *Daily News*.

Let the courts throw open the door to all well-considered scientific discoveries. Modern science has made it possible to look beneath the tissues of the human body, and has aided surgery in telling of the hidden mysteries. We believe it to be our duty in this case to be the first, if you please to so consider it, in admitting in evidence a process known and acknowledged as a determinate science. The exhibits will be admitted in evidence.

The judge allowed Mr. Buckwalter to bring X-ray equipment into the courtroom. The fascinated crowd watched as one strange-looking object after another was brought in. One of Smith's lawyers, Ben B. Lindsey, later described the scene:

We offered to show the jury the bones in their hands which created such terrific excitement about the court house that extra bailiffs were called in to keep the court in order during the argument. The excitement was intense, the "gallery" on my side restrained from breaking into applause on several occasions because of their anxiety to have this "miracle" demonstrated and actually recognized by a court.

Smith's lawyers showed the court an X-ray of a hand, then one of a normal femur, and finally the X-ray of Smith's femur that clearly showed his bone was broken. It was hard for the defense to argue against such evidence.

In another court case, X-rays were used in Cincinnati, Ohio, in late December 1896 as a sort of lie detector. A young man was arrested for injuring a co-worker. He told the police officer he was nineteen years old. Later, the boy's father realized his son would be tried in criminal court as an adult. So he claimed the boy was really only seventeen years old. The juvenile court doctor didn't believe him.

Scientific American reported:

Thoroughly convinced that the youth was at least 18 years old, the juvenile court physician decided to have x-ray photographs made of the epiphyseal bones of his hand, elbow, and hip, and also photos of the same bones of a 17 year old youth. Comparison, it was hoped, would then settle the matter, as it is a known fact in medical circles that when a boy reaches the age of 18 years those bones become hardened. The photographs developed from the x-ray pictures of the bones of the boys showed that those of the 17 year old boy had not hardened but those of the defendant in the case had done so. The physician immediately fixed the age of the prisoner at 18 years or more.

A murder trial in Elmira, New York, in 1897 ended with a different twist. George Orme had shot James Punzo in the head, but Punzo didn't die immediately. The doctor tried unsuccessfully to find the bullet that had lodged in his brain with a probe. The patient appeared to be getting better, and about three weeks after the shooting, a search for the bullet was attempted using X-rays. Punzo was put to sleep with ether, a medicine that makes the patient unconscious, and exposed to X-rays for thirty-five minutes. The resulting film was poor in quality and only showed a slight outline of the skull. It was not adequately exposed to show the location of the bullet.

A few hours after the attempted X-ray, Punzo took a turn for the worse, and twelve days later he died. At the trial, Mr. Orme's lawyers claimed Mr. Punzo did not die of the bullet wound alone, but also from the ether and X-rays.

The jury fell for it and let Orme go free.

In another case, a man had broken his arm when he was a child. His wrist didn't heal properly and became permanently disfigured. When he found out about X-rays, he had one taken of his deformed arm. The film showed that the doctor had not set the bone in the correct position years before. The man was quoted in the *British Journal of Photography* as saying,

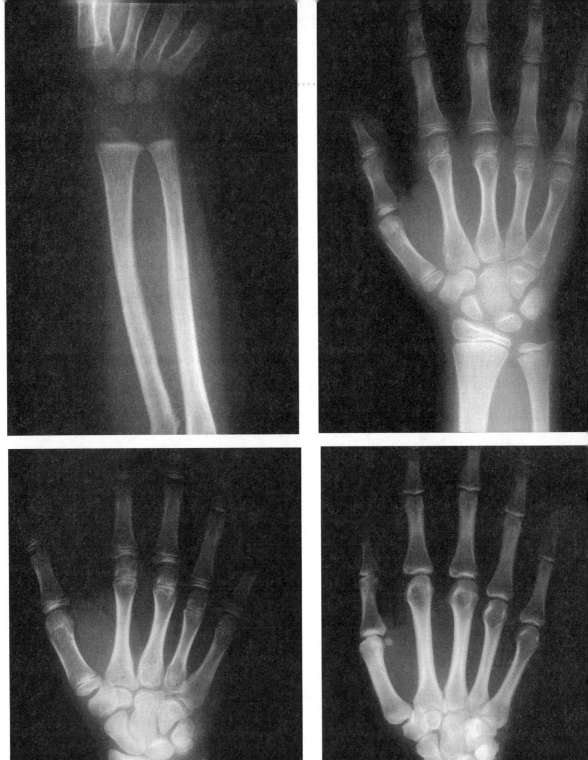

"It's a good thing for him that the surgeon who set my arm is dead, otherwise I would certainly take action against him."

The discovery of X-rays forever changed the way medical legal cases would be argued. A surefire way to prove that doctors sometimes misdiagnosed their patients was found at last.

FACING PAGE: When babies are born, they have about 350 bones—many more than they will have as adults. This is because several of a child's small bones grow together to become one adult bone. At birth, most of these aren't true bones yet; they are made of cartilage, like the soft, movable tip of your nose. As a baby grows, the cartilage ossifies—changes into bone. Located near each end of long bones like those in the arms and legs, there are areas of cartilage called epiphyses that will eventually join with the long bones. This process enables children to grow taller, and it normally takes place all through childhood and into the teenage years. Girls' bones usually harden and grow together by the time they are sixteen, and most boys' by about eighteen. At adulthood the total number of bones has decreased to 206. These X-ray images demonstrate what the epiphyses of the wrist look like at different ages as they grow together. TOP LEFT: Wrist of a twenty-month-old girl. Though only two wrist bones can be seen, all the others are there as cartilage, which doesn't show up on X-rays. You can also see a small circle above one of the long bones—this is the epiphysis of the radius bone. TOP RIGHT: Wrist of a nine-year-old girl. By now, all the wrist cartilage has turned to bone. Notice that the ends of the bones look as if they have a segment that is not attached—these are the epiphyses. She still has a lot of growing to do. BOTTOM LEFT: Wrist of a thirteen-year-old boy. You can still see the epiphyses in his hand, but notice how much bigger the wrist bones are. BOTTOM RIGHT: Wrist of a seventeen-year-old girl. You can't see any more segments near the long bones as you could in the films of the younger children. This means all her bones have completely grown together, and her wrist bones are fully developed.

5 BURNED AND BALD

People who worked with X-rays in the early days found their equipment was unreliable. Many times after a patient held still for an X-ray exposure of more than an hour, the film would not have an image on it after it was developed. When a film was blank, it meant the tube was not producing X-rays at all. Since X-rays can't be seen, heard, felt, or smelled, the workers had no way of knowing whether the tube was working until they developed the film.

The problem usually wasn't the X-ray tube; it was that control over the electric current was unstable. If the voltage going into the tube wasn't high enough, the tube could not produce X-rays.

Radiographers, people who worked with X-rays, soon developed a simple way to test their machines to make sure they were producing X-rays. First thing every morning, then periodically throughout the day, they would put their hand in front of the X-ray tube and look at it through a fluoroscope. If they saw a clear image of the bones in their own hand, they knew their equipment was ready to work. If they didn't see their bones, they knew the voltage needed adjusting.

X-ray workers didn't know it, but they were endangering their lives when they did this quick tube check by exposing themselves to high doses of

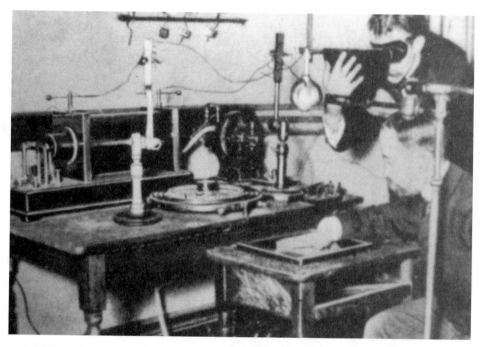

Dr. William Morton checks the strength of the X-rays coming from the tube by looking at his own hand through a fluoroscope before he takes a film of his patient's hand. This was a common practice for X-ray workers in 1896, when this photo was taken. Notice that Dr. Morton's hand is even closer to the tube than is the patient's hand.

radiation. These pioneers didn't protect themselves from X-rays at all because they had no way of knowing that the wonderful rays were dangerous.

Nor did early X-ray workers know how much radiation to use on their patients. They had to learn by making mistakes. The first telltale sign was patients' skin reactions. If they were overexposed, their skin turned red, as if sunburned. Since the medical word "erythema" means an abnormal reddening of the skin, the amount of radiation it took for skin to turn red became known as the erythema dose. Some hospitals even determined the erythema dose of their machines by exposing someone to X-rays for the sole purpose of seeing how long it took for their skin to redden. X-ray workers and doctors used the erythema dose for many years, but it wasn't a consistent, specific amount of radiation. In fact, it couldn't be calculated as a scientific measurement at all because there were variations in the strength of the X-rays each machine produced, and each person differed in the amount of radiation he could get before his skin turned red. (The same principle would apply to people lying on a beach: a person with light skin will turn red from sunburn much faster than one with darker skin.) Although the erythema dose was not an exact term, it was the best one the early experimenters had to describe an amount of radiation.

A radiologist sits under a specially designed X-ray table in Paris in 1898. While he looks at the patient's chest area with a fluoroscope, his entire body is being exposed to the radiation that is streaming through the patient.

During the first few years, radiographers examined their patients with a fluoroscope more often than they took permanent X-ray films. To use the fluoroscope, they held it close to the patient to see the image that appeared on the screen when the X-rays were turned on. When the exam was over, the image was gone. A fluoroscope exam didn't leave a permanent record.

The result was that the radiographer, who usually stood right beside the patient, was exposed to almost as much radiation as each of his patients. For example, if he X-rayed ten patients every day for five days, at the end of only one week he would have exposed himself to fifty doses of radiation. After only a few months of working with X-rays, most radiographers noticed their hands were red, almost as if they were sunburned. No one knew why.

Soon horror stories about damage done to radiographers and patients began to trickle into the media.

John Daniel, a physicist at Vanderbilt University in Nashville, Tennessee, reported a peculiar incident that happened on February 29, 1896. He had been asked to take a skull X-ray of a boy who had been accidentally shot, but he wasn't sure his equipment was capable of producing one. Dr. William Dudley volunteered to be the guinea pig to test Daniel's machine.

Mr. Daniel exposed Dr. Dudley for one hour with the X-ray tube placed one-half inch from the man's head. But when the film was developed, it did not have an image on it. They assumed the equipment was not able to show the skull successfully. Three weeks later, a circle of hair two inches wide fell out of Dudley's head on the side that had been nearest the X-ray tube. Neither of them could imagine why.

When newspapers first reported how a patient's hair fell out after being exposed to X-rays, it seemed almost funny to many people. In response to these reports, *The Lancet*, a British medical periodical, jokingly predicted that the new rays might replace shaving for men. They suggested that men

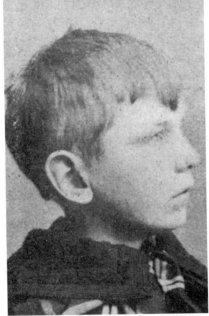

could irradiate their faces each night and wash away their whiskers the next morning.

One Frenchman heard about this unexpected result of X-ray treatments and hatched a scheme to make himself rich, while at the same time doing the ladies of his country a favor. Monsieur Gaudoin opened an X-ray business in Paris. *The British Journal of Photography* reported the story:

He was aware that a considerable proportion of his country-women are endowed with soft, silky moustaches, which are by no means appreciated by marriageable young girls and even married ladies. He resolved, therefore, to use the roentgen rays as a *dépilatoire*, to remove the superfluous hair from their lips and, when needful, from their chins. Having discreetly made known his benevolent inten-

Some people reported that their hair fell out after being exposed to X-rays. This boy was exposed to X-rays for forty minutes with the tube eighteen inches from his head to get an X-ray of his skull. TOP: About three weeks later, the hair on the side nearest the tube suddenly fell out. BOTTOM: Four months later, the boy's new hair had grown back normally.

tion, he was not long in securing fair customers. They flocked into his laboratory, patiently waiting their turn, cheerfully paid their fees and received the invisible rays on their full-blown moustaches and incipient beards. But these appendages made no sign of vanishing, and some ladies who had been under the treatment asked to have their money back. M. Gaudoin appeased these infuriated graces and hurriedly retired from the business with the fees he had accumulated.

Monsieur Gaudoin must have been more successful at attracting customers than he was at operating his X-ray equipment, since his treatments didn't work. And when the ladies who once flocked into his laboratory wanted to flock back out with their money in their purses, the once-charming Monsieur Gaudoin did the vanishing act himself that he couldn't do for the ladies' mustaches.

In Berlin, Germany, a seventeen-year-old boy got a job demonstrating X-rays during the early summer of 1896. Once or twice a day for four weeks, he used his own body to show off the rays' powers to an audience. Each session lasted about ten minutes.

Everything went well until the boy began to have problems with his skin. He went to his doctor, Dr. Macuse, who described his condition in this way:

The part of his face which was turned toward the tube, and which therefore was first struck by the rays, showed a diffuse reddening with a brownish discoloration which covered the whole half of the face. The discoloration was darkest at his ear. . . . The young man first noticed the change in his face two weeks after the beginning of his experiments when he looked into the mirror. He tried to regain his normal appearance by washing the face with vinegar, but the only result was that the skin part of the face "came off in large pieces." The first observation of the changes in his face did not prevent him from continuing his experiments, for the reddening [became less] marked . . . and was thought to be harmless. A few days later, however, it was necessary to discontinue the experiments on account of the damage to the skin, and in the following five days, during which I observed him, I noticed that the reddening of the face decreased considerably. For some unknown reasons, the patient has not come back to see me since then.

The *Münchener Medizinische Wochenschrift*, a journal from Munich, Germany, reported this young man's case but didn't believe X-rays were the cause of his skin damage. It wrote: "The dermatitis, slight burn of the skin and alopecia [baldness] which were observed on a young man who was employed to demonstrate the effect of X-ray, are probably due to an effect of the high tension currents which go from the tube to the body and not to the direct effect of radiation."

A similar experience happened to Herbert Hawks, a student at Columbia University in New York City. When Hawks heard the news of the discovery of X-rays, he built his own machine to conduct experiments and also volunteered in the new X-ray laboratory at the university.

During the summer of 1896, he got a job demonstrating X-rays at Bloomingdale's department store in New York. He ran his X-ray machine for as long as two hours at a time for curious customers. To show what it could do, Hawks would put his hand in the X-ray beam so the bones could be seen. Sometimes he placed his head in the X-ray beam to show his audience the movements of his jawbone as he opened and closed his mouth.

In early July, after only four days on the job, Hawks noticed some changes in his body. He described his condition in *The Electrical Engineer* of September 16, 1896:

> At the end of a few days I found that the rays were having quite an effect upon me. At first the skin began to dry and to itch, all the moisture having been taken out of it. . . . After a little longer exposure my hand, which was the part most exposed, began to swell, the inflammation being in the hand for about ten days; at the end of that time the swelling rapidly went away, but the skin all came off, just as with a sunburn. The joints and finger nails seemed to suffer most, the joints becoming nearly transparent, and the nails killed, as new nails have since grown. Wherever the hair was exposed to the ray it fell out, but it does not seem to be permanently injured as it grows again as the skin gradually returns to a healthy condition, but the growth is very slow. In my case it was eight weeks after the exposure before it started to grow. The eyes were also very badly affected, where not covered by the lids. The exposure to produce such effects as these probably amounted to between two and three hours.

The problems with his hands grew worse. He took two weeks off from his demonstration job and went to the doctor. His doctor advised him to protect his hands by smearing petroleum jelly on them and wearing gloves when he worked with X-rays. He returned to work, but these things didn't help. Then he tried covering his hand with tinfoil, but that didn't work either.

Hawks thought the damage was caused not by X-rays but by exposure to high-voltage electricity. However, his skin condition did not improve until he stopped working with X-rays altogether.

It was fortunate that Herbert Hawks's frequent overexposure to X-rays didn't kill him. He was still alive thirty-eight years later and described his health in a letter to a researcher:

My hand recovered and has since been in good shape except for the peculiar scarred effects coming from such burns. The skin is a little bit thicker than normal skin but there is no discomfort. *My nails on both hands came off*—in fact the nail on the index finger of the right hand came off four times, and for a considerable time the cuticle continued to grow out over the nails and had to be periodically cut off. I still have all of the nails on my right hand, but they are rather brittle and the skin or tissue under the nails is not exactly normal as it becomes easily stained and hard to clean.

In 1896, another case of injury was reported. Ten years earlier, a bank robber had shot William Levy of Eau Claire, Wisconsin, in the head. The bullet had been lodged there ever since. Through the years Levy wondered where exactly the bullet was and if it could be removed. At last, the discovery of X-rays made it possible to find out.

He asked Professor Fred Jones of the Physical Laboratory at the University of Minnesota to examine his head with X-rays. Professor Jones warned him that taking films of his head might cause his hair to fall out, but Levy insisted on the X-rays anyway. A report in *Electrical Review* said he "came up and sat from 8 o'clock in the morning till 10 at night for a Roentgen-ray picture of his head." Several exposures were taken, for one of which the X-ray tube was placed inside his mouth. These clearly showed the bullet was lodged near the back of his skull.

"The next day," the report continued,

Mr. Levy began to notice a peculiar effect on his skin wherever it had been most exposed to the rays, and the hair on the right side of his head, which had been near the wire, began to fall out. In a few days the right side of his head was perfectly bald, his right ear had swollen to twice its natural size and presented the same appearance as if very badly frozen. Sores were visible on his head, his mouth and throat were blistered so that he could not eat solid food for three weeks, and his lips were swollen, cracked and bleeding. In fact, the long exposure to the X rays, while giving him no pain at the time, seemed to have produced very similar effects to a very severe burn.

Even these horrible results didn't stop Mr. Levy. The report concluded: "Mr. Levy has recovered from the effects of his burns, but he still has half a bald head. He is a plucky man, about 30 years of age, and intends to have the investigations carried further and the bullet removed. He has already written to Professor Jones, asking for another sitting."

Throughout 1896 story after story was reported about damage people suffered after working with or sitting for X-rays. Toward the end of the year, Professor Elihu Thomson, a physicist working at the General Electric Laboratory in Schenectady, New York, decided to perform a little experiment to find out for himself if the X-rays themselves were causing the problem. He would expose a part of his own body for the test. Since he realized the X-rays could be harmful, he thought about which body part he could live without if damage occurred. After careful consideration, he decided to use the last joint of the little finger on his left hand. (A good choice, especially if you are right-handed.)

Thomson described the test and how it affected his finger in November 1896, in both *The Electrical Engineer* and *Electrical World*:

> After exposing the little finger of my left hand for one half hour close to the tube at about 1½ in. . . . , no decided effect followed until over a week; that finger then reddened, became extremely sensitive, swollen, stiff, and to a certain extent painful. I wish to add that at present about seventeen days have elapsed since the exposure and the finger is still quite sore but showing signs of improvement. Two-thirds of the exposed portion is covered by a large blister which becomes larger every day. . . . There is evidently a point beyond which exposure cannot go without causing serious trouble.

He proved to himself that the damage was a direct result of the X-ray exposure. "The evidence . . . leads me to think that the effect is another indication of the chemical activity of roentgen rays." The professor ended with a wise warning: "Do not expose more than one finger; . . . or there may be cause for regret when too late."

Even though Thomson was convinced of the possible danger of the rays, many disagreed with him. Others suggested various theories about what was causing the skin damage instead of X-rays, such as strong electric currents, chemicals used to develop film, cathode rays, ultraviolet rays, bacteria driven into the skin by the X-rays, or simply human mistakes.

Professor Thomson's claim that X-rays were causing damage was eventually proved correct. After harming his finger, Thomson used caution when he worked with the rays. He was one of the few early X-ray researchers still alive thirty-three years later to report on his injury: "I bear the scar of this burn now. . . . It sometimes troubles me in the winter by cracking open and chapping."

The first person known to have died because of his work with X-rays was Clarence Dally. He was Thomas Edison's assistant and worked with him to develop the fluoroscope. It was Dally who kept the fluoroscope machine running smoothly at Edison's public exhibition in New York City.

After Edison and Dally perfected the fluoroscope, they began plans for a fluorescent X-ray lamp. This lamp was to be an electric lightbulb that used X-rays to illuminate it. Dally was a glassblower who made each glass X-ray lamp by hand. During the process of sealing and testing these lamps, he was exposed to enormous

Clarence Dally worked on sealing the Edison X-ray fluorescent lamps. He would be the first person known to die as a result of overexposure to X-rays.

amounts of radiation. This radiation was in addition to the heavy doses he received while he worked on the fluoroscope.

Dally checked the output of the X-ray tube by looking at his left hand through the fluoroscope, so the first sign of damage was that his left hand became red, swollen, and painful. When it got really bad, he'd stop working for a few days until it was a little better. But then he went right back to doing the same thing. Eventually, his left hand hurt so badly that he began using his right hand to check the tube. Another sign of his overexposure to X-rays was that the hair on the front part of his head fell out, and so did his eyebrows and eyelashes.

After Thomas Edison saw the effect the X-rays had on Dally, he wrote, "I started in to make a number of these lamps, but I soon found that the X-ray *had affected poisonously my assistant, Mr. Dally*, so that his hair came out and his flesh commenced to ulcerate. I then concluded it would not do, and that it would not be a very popular kind of light, so I dropped it."

Thomas Edison sits under the glow of his X-ray fluorescent lamp in 1896. He stopped developing these lamps when he realized that Clarence Dally, his assistant, was injured from working on them.

It was too late for Clarence Dally. Serious damage had been done in the years he worked with X-rays. By 1902, Dally was suffering horrible pain from the burns on his left hand. An oozing sore the size of a playing card on the back of his left wrist would not go away. Doctors repeatedly took skin from his leg and grafted it onto his wrist to try to get it to heal. It never worked. Finally a surgeon had to amputate the hand. Dally's right hand had X-ray damage, too; four fingers and part of his right palm were amputated.

Even these drastic measures didn't help. The deep X-ray burns turned into cancer. His doctors tried everything to stop the spread of his disease, even exposing him to more X-rays to see if that would help. Dally's right arm was amputated at the shoulder and his left arm at the elbow in an attempt to arrest the stubborn cancer. He was in constant pain.

Clarence Dally was thirty-nine years old when he died in 1904. Although he was the first person to experience the slow, agonizing death resulting from radiation sickness, he would not be the last.

Dr. Frederick Baetjer, who became the Professor of Roentgenology at Johns Hopkins Hospital in Baltimore, Maryland, endured more than one hundred operations for his own X-ray-induced injuries. He described how the burns felt: "The pain is most intense and is best described as a sharp, shooting neuralgic pain of the worst character. It lasts two or three seconds and occurs from eight to ten times every minute."

Dr. John Pitkin of Buffalo, New York, described his pain like this: "Extreme tenderness to the slightest touch; hot and cold waves and flashes; warmth, tingling, pricking, throbbing, stinging, crawling, boring and burning sensations, as if the parts were on fire." He was one of the lucky ones. He lived with this pain for another thirty-two years after this statement.

Many didn't live long with their radiation injuries, including one of the first women pioneers in X-rays—Elizabeth Fleischmann. When Dr. Roentgen discovered X-rays, she was working as a bookkeeper and living in San Francisco with her sister and her sister's husband, who was a doctor. Both Fleischmann and her brother-in-law were fascinated by X-rays. She was so interested in them that at the age of thirty-nine she quit her job and took a six-month course in electrical science.

In 1897, she borrowed money from her father to buy X-ray equipment and had it installed in her brother-in-law's office, which was located in their home. He and Fleishmann were eager to see what could be done with their new equipment. They took turns taking X-rays of each other. Their skin soon showed signs of burns, but it didn't stop them.

When the Spanish-American War broke out in 1898, Fleishmann began taking X-rays of wounded soldiers. Her reputation as a radiographer grew because the doctors could always count on her to get films of excellent quality that showed bone injuries and the exact location of bullets. Her work was so good that she was officially praised by the surgeon general of the United States Army.

After the war Fleishmann continued working twelve hours a day in her X-ray lab. She often placed her own body in the X-ray beam to show her patients they didn't need to be afraid. She assured them the rays were painless and harmless. Fleishmann never changed the way she worked or tried to protect herself from the damaging rays, even after reports of X-ray damage were printed in the newspapers.

Years of overexposure eventually caught up with Fleishmann. Her hands became dry and cracked. Sores and warts developed on her fingers. When her injuries became cancerous and spread, her arm and shoulder had to be amputated. But it was too late to save Fleishmann's life. The cancer

Elizabeth Fleischmann, one of many women who worked with X-rays in the early days, examines a patient with a fluoroscope. She opened one of the first X-ray clinics in the state of California.

continued to spread throughout her body. She died in 1905 at the age of forty-six.

Case after case of sickness and death from overexposure to X-rays were reported in the news. Yet many ignored the warnings. While some people pushed for safety standards to protect workers and patients, others resisted them.

Dr. Rome Wagner and his brother, Dr. Thurman Wagner, built X-ray equipment in Chicago. Both of them exposed themselves to X-rays when they demonstrated their machines to groups of doctors. It didn't take long for burns and sores to appear on their skin. Their sister wrote about how they handled the great pain of their injuries: "Everything was always regarded as a joke, but if it had not been, we could not have borne it. When their suffering was greatest they walked the floor and sang a popular song or took a long walk. . . . They never allowed themselves to become discouraged. There were so many things they must do, that they did not give themselves time to think of their own condition."

Even after they had severe radiation damage, they continued to work with X-rays. But Rome's injuries did make him consider ways he might protect himself from further harm. He created a test to determine if his body had been exposed to any radiation during the workday. He reasoned that since X-rays exposed film to produce an image, he could use that to his advantage. He carried a piece of film in his pocket, knowing that if any radiation reached the film, he could tell after it was developed. At the end of each day, he developed the film, which would indicate whether or not he had been exposed.

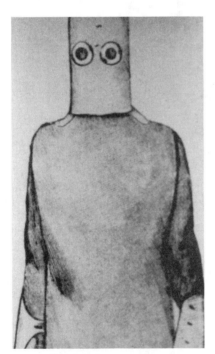

An early lead apron used to protect X-ray workers from overexposure. The apron and strange-looking helmet must have been heavy and hot to wear.

His attempts to protect himself from X-rays came too late. He had already developed cancer in his hands and cheek. Rome died of radiation-induced injuries in 1908, and his brother, Thurman, died in 1912. But Rome Wagner's last attempt at radiation protection lives on. Today, all people who work with radiation wear a piece of film clipped to their clothes, just as Dr. Wagner did. This dosimeter, or "film badge," is used to record the amount of radiation each worker receives, to prevent overexposure.

Dr. Mihran Kassabian of Philadelphia learned much of what he knew about X-rays from working with them during the Spanish-American War. He was considered an expert on X-rays and wrote many articles and books on the subject. Like most doctors in the first few years of the X-ray, Dr. Kassabian examined more of his patients with a handheld fluoroscope than

Dr. Mihran Kassabian examines a patient with a fluoroscope in his X-ray laboratory at a Philadelphia hospital in 1901. He wrote a textbook on the subject of X-rays and was considered to be an expert medical witness about X-rays in court cases.

he did by taking X-ray films. If his patients were nervous about having an X-ray made, he would assure them there was nothing to be afraid of by showing them his own left hand through the fluoroscope before he exposed them. He wrote that doing this "tends to prevent the patient becoming emotional or excited."

His medical practice had exposed him to large amounts of radiation. By April 1900, damage appeared on his left hand. For a month his fingers were red, then "the itching became intense, the skin became tough, glossy, edematous [full of fluid] and yellow." This was only the beginning of the ten years of pain and misery his injury caused him. "In order to effect a cure of my hands," he wrote, "I have used every remedial agent mentioned in all the text-books on skin diseases. . . . I have been unfortunate in finding a remedy to cure my hands."

Dr. Kassabian took photographs of his hands through the years to show how the rays had damaged them. He hoped others would learn from his experience and be spared the same damage. He studied and wrote about X-rays until his death from radiation-induced cancer in 1910.

Even after it became known that overexposure to X-rays was dangerous, some people continued to misuse them. As late as the 1920s, companies in America used X-rays to get rid of women's unwanted facial hair. Since the public knew about the risks of radiation, these businesses never advertised or described their treatments as using X-rays. Instead they used words like "Short Wave Treatment," "Epilax Ray," and "Light Treatment."

The best-known of these businesses was the Tricho System, developed by Dr. Albert C. Geyser, a New York City physician. Seventy-five "Tricho machines" were in use in the United States and Canada by 1925.

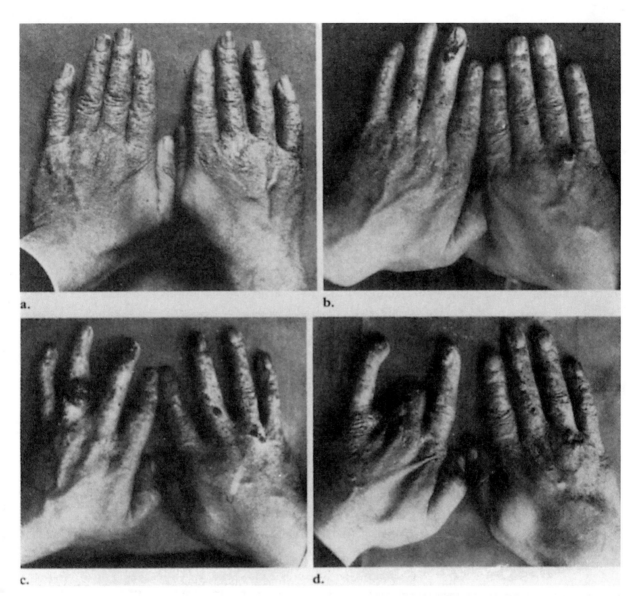

These photographs show the progression of damage to Dr. Mihran Kassabian's hands over a six-year period. More damage is seen on his left hand, which he would often use to check the X-ray tube to see if it was functioning properly. (a) 1903. (b) January 1908. (c) April 1909. (d) September 1909.

Advertisements for the Tricho System assured the public that physicians and beauty experts endorsed the system. They also guaranteed that the removal of facial hair with their system was safe and painless and would not leave a scar. The advertisements did not mention that the "system" was really an X-ray machine.

Dr. Geyser leased his Tricho machines to beauty shops and gave beauticians a two-week course on how to operate them. The clients would receive a treatment every two weeks that lasted for a few minutes. Their facial hair usually fell out by the sixth visit. The women then received more treatments to prevent the hair from growing back. The entire therapy averaged about twenty sessions, although some women may have had as many as ninety. Thousands and thousands of women across the county had these beauty treatments. In New York City alone, the Tricho System treated 20,000 women within the first six years of operation.

Dr. Geyser understood the danger of X-rays but believed they were safe when given in small doses over a long period of time. In 1925, an article appeared in *The Business Survey* that praised his treatments:

Early attempts to remove hair from the face by means of the X-ray resulted in inflammation and sores, and the method fell into disrepute until the perfection of the Tricho System by Dr. Geyser. Even now, with the flawlessness and harmlessness of its results so widely demonstrated, some prejudice against it still remains. This is being dispelled gradually, however, and in due time disfiguring superfluous hair on the faces of women will be unknown.

The damage these treatments caused sometimes took years to show up. However, problems for one young woman from Milwaukee were quick to surface. Her case was described this way:

[She had] . . . nineteen Tricho treatments between July, 1926 and September, 1927. In October, 1927, patient first observed redness and itching, which increased in severity, resulting in painful ulceration and disability. By December, 1928, ulcers and other painful changes were present on hands, forearms, and legs, knees. . . . Patient wholly disabled for work, bedridden, and suffering severely.

This is one woman among thousands who received "beauty treatments" to get rid of unwanted facial hair. She didn't understand these treatments were actually exposing her to X-rays. Women all over America and the world paid for these treatments, but they got more than they bargained for. Many of them got gum disease, sores, scars, X-ray burns, skin cancers, and sometimes a painful, premature death.

When stories of horrible suffering and sometimes death caused by these beauty treatments were reported, the parlors gradually stopped offering them. Most women who were injured didn't sue anyone because they didn't want the publicity. The American Medical Association judged the Tricho System to be unsafe in 1929.

About twenty years later, two doctors who researched these injuries reported in *The Journal of the American Medical Association* that "the number of cases of x-ray burns, cancer and death resulting from treatments administered by the Tricho Institute must have run into the thousands. It is impossible to obtain or estimate the actual number because the cases were not recorded."

Safety precautions were slow in coming. For years there had been no guidelines to protect people from the harmful effects of radiation. It wasn't until 1928 in Stockholm, Sweden, more than thirty years after the discovery of X-rays, that the International Congress of Radiology agreed upon a system to measure radiation that could be used uniformly all over the world. It invented a unit of radiation called a "roentgen." At last, there was a common term that could be used when discussing amounts of X-ray exposure. This group also suggested safety guidelines for the first time at this meeting.

These guidelines came too late for many early X-ray workers. In 1936, a monument dedicated to the memory of the men and women who died as a result of their work with X-rays was placed in the courtyard of St. Georg Hospital in Hamburg, Germany. The names of 168 people from all over the world were engraved on the side of the square stone. The inscription reads:

To the Röntgenologists and Radiologists of All Nations, Doctors, Physicists, Chemists, Technical Workers, Laboratory Workers, and Hospital Sisters who gave their lives in the struggle against the diseases of mankind. They were heroic leaders in the development of the successful and safe use of Röntgen rays and radium in medicine. Immortal is the glory of the work of the dead.

Antoine Béclère, an eighty-one-year-old French radiologist (a doctor who specializes in reading X-rays), spoke at the stone's dedication ceremony. He said:

> All these victims acquitted their task, humble or exalted, and with the same devotion. All have acquired equal merit, all have equal right to honor. These noble martyrs did not speak the same lan-

The martyrs' memorial stone placed in the courtyard of the St. Georg Hospital in Hamburg, Germany. It is inscribed with the names of nearly four hundred people who died as a result of working with radiation.

guage, did not belong to the same country, they were of different races and religions. . . . They were all devoted to the mission of fighting, at the peril of their lives, the same enemies, illness and suffering, with the aid of the marvelous weapon which Röntgen gave to medicine, without fear that this weapon was double-edged and, wielded, as it was, without the precautions now in use, would one day wound and kill them.

The names of more than two hundred other people who died as a result of their work with X-rays have been added to the monument since that day.

6 SCHEMES AND DREAMS

The public was amazed by X-rays and came up with all sorts of ideas about how they might be used. But some of these ideas had about as much chance for success as having a snowball fight in the desert.

When the newspapers first wrote about how powerful X-rays were, it caused some people to worry that the rays could destroy cities. Others wondered if they could be used on criminals to stop their bad behavior. Or perhaps X-rays would be able to capture our thoughts and dreams. Some wondered if X-rays could be used to read the inside of a letter without opening it. Still others suggested X-rays would reveal the secrets of gravity. One article in *The New York Times* predicted that "X-rays, that is invisible rays, will in the future play an important part in the lighting of our houses and streets."

Some people were convinced X-rays could unlock the secrets of nature. The ability of X-rays to make fluorescent material glow was compared to the glow of fireflies and glowworms because they all gave off a mysterious light. Researchers studied these insects with X-rays to see if they could find out what made them glow. It remained a mystery.

Dr. William Morton hoped autopsies would no longer be needed, since X-ray images taught doctors more about human anatomy and the workings of internal organs than had ever been known before. But that didn't happen; autopsies are still necessary and are frequently done today. Another idea was to use X-rays to see whether or not a person was dead. I don't know about you, but I wouldn't want to go to a doctor who was iffy on this life-or-death question.

John Mandel, a professor at Columbia College in New York, found something else X-rays could not do. He conducted experiments to see if X-rays could restore life to animals who had drowned. To test his theory, he killed four mice and one snake and exposed them to X-rays. When the rays did not bring them back to life, he reported that "all the experiments with the rays failed to produce any results." The professor's deduction came a bit too late for the mice and snake.

The truth about what X-rays could and could not do didn't stand in the way of some outrageous claims. Some people said their eyes were so sensitive to X-rays that they could actually see through objects. Others claimed blind people could see by using X-rays. One woman said she had a lot of pain in her broken ankle, but after she had X-rays taken of it, all the pain, swelling, and soreness went away. Thomas Edison once received a letter from someone who wanted to buy "one pound of X-rays." Another package contained a pair of empty opera glasses with instructions to "fit them with X-rays." These last two orders still haven't been filled.

Mr. Ingles Rogers claimed he could make an image similar to an X-ray by staring at a photographic plate in the dark. Others said they could produce an image just by thinking of a certain object. A report from Columbia College said that when "the shadow of a bone was projected with X-rays on the brain of a dog, he immediately became hungry." This one would be hard to prove, since my dog is always hungry—isn't yours?

Another impossible nugget was reported in a newspaper in Cedar Rapids, Iowa:

> George Johnson . . . who has been experimenting with the X-rays, thinks that he has made a discovery that will startle the world. By means of what he called the X-rays he is enabled to change in three hours' time a cheap piece of metal worth about 13 cents to $153 worth of gold. The metal so transformed has been tested and pronounced pure gold.

In reality, George Johnson's method of making gold didn't pan out.

A medical school claimed they were using X-rays to "reflect anatomic diagrams directly into the brains of advanced medical students, making a much more enduring impression than ordinary teaching methods." If only this were possible, school would be a lot easier, wouldn't it?

Any mention of X-rays was an attention-getter in the early days and was sometimes used in advertisements—whether the claim was possible or not. A detective in London claimed to use X-rays in his business. He ran an advertisement in the London *Standard* that read: "The New Photography— Owing to the success Mr. Henry Slater has personally achieved with the New Photography, he is prepared to introduce same in divorce matters free of charge." No one could ever figure out exactly how Mr. Slater planned to use X-rays in divorce cases, probably not even Mr. Slater.

However, there were some suggestions for using X-rays that were reasonable and made a lot of sense—they just didn't work out quite as hoped. Miss Francis E. Willard was the president of the Women's Christian Temperance Union, an organization that discouraged the drinking of alcohol. *The Electrical Review* quoted Miss Willard in June 1896 as saying, "I believe the X-rays are going to do much for the temperance cause. By this means drunkards and cigarette smokers can be shown the steady deterioration in their systems, which follows the practice, and seeing is believing."

Sadly, it didn't seem to make any more difference in Miss Willard's day than it has in ours.

Another good idea that didn't quite work was in the battle over vivisection. Many people in 1896—just like today—were against vivisection, which is using live animals for research purposes and sometimes hurting them in the process. Some people hoped the use of X-rays would make vivisection unnecessary. An article in *Life* magazine on February 27, 1896, said: "we are entitled to hope that it will almost put an end to vivisection. There will be no need to put a knife into a live animal when a ray will make its inner workings visible." However, using X-rays didn't decrease the use of animals for research. In the United States today, more than seventy million animals each year are used in medical, drug, cosmetic, and other types of research.

One suggestion for using X-rays was not only reasonable but way ahead of its time. A radiologist was approached by the management of a gambling hall about the possibility of using a fluoroscope to check customers for concealed weapons. About eighty years later this great idea was put to common use—as one of the security features in airports.

If the ability to detect concealed weapons had been in use for security in 1901, it could have been a great benefit to the twenty-fifth President of the United States, William McKinley. That year, an assassin fired two shots at President McKinley, one of which entered his body. Thomas Edison's laboratory received a telephone call asking him to send his X-ray machine to Buffalo, New York, to be ready in case the doctors thought the President needed an X-ray.

Clarence Dally, Edison's assistant, was one of two men who took the machine to Buffalo. They set up the equipment and waited to be called. Because President McKinley's condition was serious, they were told an X-ray would not be needed for at least a week. Dally stayed in Buffalo and the other man returned to Edison's laboratory.

In a few days, President McKinley's condition had improved so much that the doctors decided to leave the bullet in him. One of the doctors told Dally his services would not be needed. But Dally stayed in Buffalo anyway, just in case the call came that an X-ray was needed.

President McKinley's condition suddenly grew worse and he died. Since Dally could do nothing more for the slain President, he took his X-ray machine apart and prepared to leave, right after he did some sight-seeing.

President McKinley's doctors decided to conduct an autopsy. For an hour and a half, they searched his body for the bullet that killed him, but could not find it. They called for Dally to take an X-ray to locate it. But he was in nearby Niagara Falls for the day. The bullet was never recovered.

Another use for X-rays that flopped, or should I say flip-flopped, was

using them to sell children's shoes. In the late 1940s many shoe stores used a shoe-fitting fluoroscope. This was a device designed to check the fit of children's shoes by using X-rays. The X-ray tube was enclosed in a cabinet. The child, sporting new shoes, stood on a platform with his feet in the slot above the X-ray tube. When the machine was turned on, you could look down through the top of the cabinet onto the fluoroscope screen to see the child's feet inside the shoes.

Over and over, the child would try on a pair of shoes, then peek through the viewer, along with his parent, to see the X-ray image. Can you imagine how much fun it would be to wiggle your toes and see your own bones move this way and that way? It would surely be more fun than your parent saying, "Walk around and see if they slip up and down on your heel. Are you sure they fit? We aren't going to buy them unless you're sure . . ."

The problem with the shoe fluoroscope was that the customers and the salesclerks were getting more than just a fitting. Only after many years did researchers begin to study how much radiation came from these machines. A report in a 1949 issue of *The New England Journal of Medicine* concluded that "the type of radiation injury most likely to result from the unsupervised use of low-voltage fluoroscopes in shoe stores is the malformation of the feet of growing children." The authors were also concerned about the pos-

FACING PAGE: Some stores had a shoe fluoroscope like this one, which was used to see how well a pair of shoes fit. This was a deluxe model that had one viewer for the child, one for the parent, and the other for the shoe salesman. It must have been great fun to see the bones of your own feet. Do you think any kids stuck their hands into the X-ray beam? Or even better, told their little brother or sister to do it?

sibility of "injury of the blood-forming tissues of store employees." These machines were in use even into the early 1960s. They were eventually outlawed.

Through the years, some schemes people had for using X-rays failed—and sometimes their ideas were bizarre, dangerous, or simply impossible. But for every plan using X-rays that failed, many more were successful.

7 FAKE OR FACT?

Some wonderfully creative uses of X-rays have been in the world of art. X-rays themselves have influenced artists. According to an article in *Art Journal*, a group of artists in the early twentieth century known as cubists may have been partly inspired by the X-ray images they saw. Their abstract paintings sometimes showed the interior of solid objects in a way similar to the way X-rays revealed hidden structures. Some of these artists used light and shadow to create skeletonlike shapes that resemble X-rays.

But the most impressive use of X-rays in art is to uncover what has been covered up. Details revealed by an X-ray of a painting can't be seen any other way. For example, in the past, paintings were often repaired if flakes of paint fell off the canvas. These repairs cannot be seen just by looking at the painting. It takes an X-ray to detect where the repairs have been made.

An X-ray of a painting is one of the best ways to tell if it was created by a famous painter or if it is a forgery. If there is a question as to whether an old master has painted a certain painting or not, X-rays are made and compared to those of paintings that are known to be genuine. If the brush-strokes, for example, are shown to be totally different than in other work done by a certain artist, then the painting is proved to be a fake.

Since modern paints are usually made from different materials than paints of hundreds of years ago, the image they leave on an X-ray film looks different. This is one way X-rays can be used to detect a forgery. A modern artist will try to make a forgery look hundreds of years old by painting dirty varnish on it or by using artificial means to get the varnish to looked cracked. To the naked eye, the forgery may look old, but when a careful study of the X-ray image is made, the deception is obvious.

It was common many years ago for an artist to finish a painting, decide it wasn't any good, and paint a completely different picture on top of it. Or artists would paint over others' work—it was their version of recycling. Taking an X-ray is the only way to find out if there is a picture underneath the picture you see with your eyes. Sometimes museums will be more interested in the painting beneath than the one on top, and will restore the older one by having the top layer painstakingly removed.

Forgeries of rare postage stamps, like paintings, have been detected by using X-rays. Resulting films can show details such as the design of the stamp, the type of paper used, the cancellation mark, and any alterations that might have been made.

Pieces of sculpture can also be examined by X-rays to see if they are forgeries. An X-ray film of a statue can indicate how the statue was made. If the method used by the artist was one that did not exist when the statue was supposed to have been made, it is proved to be a fake. For example, a statuette of an Egyptian cat was thought to be thousands of years old until an X-ray image showed it was made of material that would not have been used

ABOVE: A well-preserved portrait painted in 1640 by Rembrandt titled *Herman Doomer*, which epitomizes Rembrandt's craft at capturing light and shadow in his work. RIGHT: An X-ray of the same painting helps historians to study Rembrandt's technique. In this detail, you can see how he used layers of white lead paint to create Doomer's ruff (collar), and how his brushstrokes on the top layer of the ruff differ from those on the lace beneath. Also notice the brushstrokes used to create the wrinkles around Doomer's eyes.

ABOVE: *Bearded Man with a Velvet Cap* was painted by Govert Flinck in about 1645. Flinck, one of Rembrandt's leading students in the 1630s, was influenced by his style and technique. By looking at this portrait, can you tell something is hidden beneath? RIGHT: An X-ray of the same painting demonstrates how canvases were sometimes recycled. A woman's image is underneath the surface paint! If you look closely, you can see the faces of both subjects: the man's nose is directly above the corner of the woman's left eye. The wide stripes that appear are the wooden supports on the back of the painting.

by ancient Egyptians. X-rays help people study sculptures in other ways, too. If a metal object is covered with corrosion, an X-ray can show the actual shape of the original piece. X-rays also reveal repairs that have been made in the past that can't be seen with the eyes.

 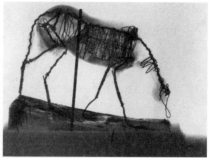

LEFT: **One of the earliest horse sculptures by Edgar Degas, *Horse at Trough*, from the early 1860s. The figure has been formed from brown wax with red highlights and rests on a wooden base. Degas's attention to detail can be especially seen in the horse's mane, mouth, and nostrils. RIGHT: An X-ray of the same sculpture shows that this attention to detail began on the inside. Degas built an intricate, almost lifelike, metal skeleton by wrapping and twisting wire before he began sculpting with wax. You can also see the nails he used to build the wooden base. Without the benefit of X-rays, we'd never be able to see the inner support for this work of art without destroying it.**

X-rays' uses aren't limited to the visual arts; they are also used in the world of music. X-ray images have made it possible to understand how the internal structures of the mouth and nose work together. This information has helped professionals perfect the mouthpieces of brass instruments so musicians can achieve the best sound.

CT (computed tomography) scans have also been used to study musical instruments. A CT scanner is a complicated X-ray machine that takes many

Not only are X-rays used to study art in many different ways, but X-rays themselves have become art. Films of everyday objects are used to make decorative items such as lampshades and night-lights.

images of an object one thin slice at a time. To better understand this imaging method, think of a loaf of sliced bread. If you took one slice of bread out of the middle of the loaf, you would see what the inside of the loaf looked like at that one exact place. A CT scan enables doctors and researchers to look at numerous cross sections (the "slices") of an object in order to evaluate the whole thing (the "loaf").

Dr. Steven Sirr, a radiologist in Minneapolis, Minnesota, performs CT scans on more than his patients. He also takes these X-ray images of Stradivarius violins. The world-famous violins were made more than two hundred fifty years ago and are still considered to be the best in the world. His scans show wormholes, cracks, and even areas that were patched long ago. The films also give instrument

X-ray images of a violin made in 1720 in Cremona, Italy, by the famous maker Antonio Stradivari. Today, the instrument is owned by a wealthy amateur violinist who plays it every day. RIGHT: A traditional X-ray. The parallel lines mark the places where the CT scan will take images. Each image will be 3 millimeters thick (about an eighth of an inch). BELOW, LEFT: A CT image through the top of the violin lengthwise. You can see the *f*-shaped resonance holes. The small white rectangles are internal pieces of wood used to repair cracks in the front plate. BELOW, RIGHT: A crosswise section of the violin in about the middle of it. The gaps in the outline are where the resonance holes are.

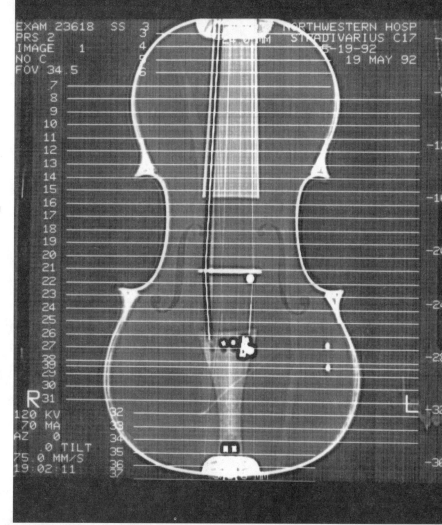

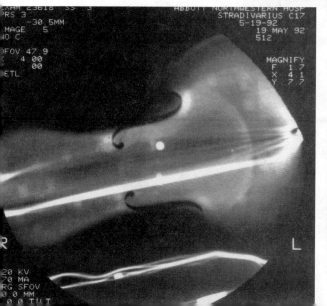

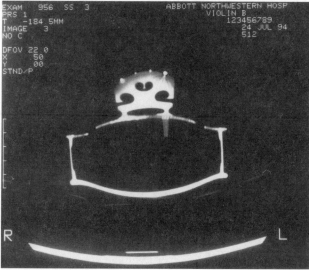

Superman uses his X-ray vision to see through the side of a briefcase and foil a villainous plot.

makers a glimpse into the construction skills of the master violin makers of the past.

However, X-rays are not always used so seriously. One of the best-known superheroes of all has the benefit of X-ray vision any time he wants it, along with a few other super-abilities such as leaping tall buildings in a single bound and being faster than a speeding bullet. And who is this super-hero who has devoted himself to helping those in need? Look! Up in the sky! It's a bird! It's a plane! It's Super-man! His X-ray vision is a big help as he fights evil in Me-tropolis.

It seems X-rays have influenced almost every area of life. Not only science and medicine but art and culture have been forever altered by them. Today, X-ray images are so familiar to us that they appear in

COPYRIGHT TRACOMIR

instant X-ray sight

X-ray 'spec's that give you the amazing illusion to see right through everything you look at! See the bones in your hands, the yolk in an egg, the lead in a pencil and . . . the most amazing things, when looking at girls and friends! Especially amusing at those fun parties!

£1.75 incl. P.&P.

Order soon so as not to be disappointed. C.W.O. to:
SENE PARK PRODUCTS (SM7) LAMBERTON HOUSE, SENE PARK, HYTHE, KENT CT21 5XB.

Advertisement from a British newspaper in 1980. Notice the ad says these specs "give you the amazing illusion to see right through everything." X-ray glasses like this are not possible, but that didn't stop magazines from running ads for them for many years.

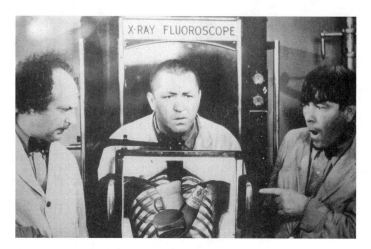

The Three Stooges got a few laughs from this impossible X-ray.

movies and television shows as part of the background. They are used in TV commercials to advertise almost any kind of product, including medicine, breakfast cereal, pillows, chiropractors, cars, and food. X-rays have become so much a part of our popular culture we don't even notice them all around us. We ignore X-ray images that one hundred years ago would have caused people to stare in wonder.

8 SECRETS REVEALED

Another area where X-rays have been a success is in studying people from the past. X-rays are perhaps the most important tool used today to examine Egyptian mummies. Before X-rays were possible, no one could see what lay hidden beneath the tightly wrapped mummies without unwrapping them. So, for many years, scientists unwound mummies to study them, but they destroyed them in the process. X-rays gave archaeologists a way to "see" inside the mummies without damaging them.

The secrets of the mummies that had been hidden beneath mysterious wrappings for centuries were at last revealed by using X-rays. Sometimes what lay under the surface surprised the archaeologists.

Without unwrapping mummies, X-rays proved to be the only way to find out about the statuettes, religious symbols, or jewelry that were sometimes placed inside the mummies' bodies or in their outer wrappings at the time of mummification. Some mummies were victims of grave robbers hundreds or thousands of years ago. X-ray films of these give evidence that robbers hacked up the mummies, breaking their bones while searching for

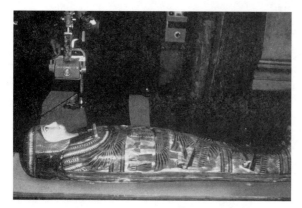 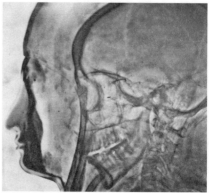

LEFT: The sarcophagus containing the mummy of an Egyptian woman from the Twenty-second Dynasty (about 950–750 B.C.) named Ta-pero. RIGHT: An X-ray shows Ta-pero's face, almost exactly under the face of the sarcophagus.

hidden treasure. One X-ray of a mummified woman shows that her burial jewelry was left in a jumble after being searched by grave robbers. The ancient thieves apparently did not think the burial jewelry worth stealing, since it was left behind.

Today, scientists are using X-rays to diagnose medical problems that troubled the Egyptians thousands of years ago. X-rays of mummies have shown evidence of clubfoot, arthritis, hardening of the arteries, old broken bones, scoliosis, polio, and tuberculosis. Sometimes films can suggest what caused the mummy's death. The X-rays of the mummy of Seqenenre Tao, a ruler of the Seventeenth Dynasty (about 1600 B.C.), showed the injuries he may have received in a battle. The films clearly indicate an ax wound to his forehead and a hole made from a blow to the head with a blunt object. Thousands of years later, it is clear that these injuries caused his death because there is no sign of any new bone growth.

X-rays can also show how old the mummified person was at the time of

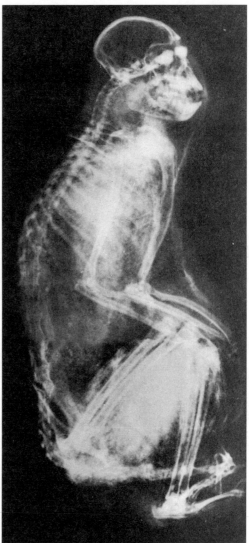

This small mummy, labeled Princess Moutemhet, was found inside the sarcophagus of Makare, a young woman who had given birth to a child not long before she died. However, when X-rays of the "baby" mummy were taken, the films proved that inside the carefully wrapped package were not the remains of a human baby but those of a female baboon.

death by showing how much wear the teeth have. The warm winds of Egypt blew sand everywhere—even into the food as it was being prepared. When the ancient Egyptians ate, they would often be chewing on small amounts of sand. This would wear down their teeth. If the teeth of an adult mummy were not worn down very much, it indicated that the person died in young adulthood. If the teeth showed some wear, the person was older at the time of death. Teeth worn down almost to the gums indicates the person died in old age.

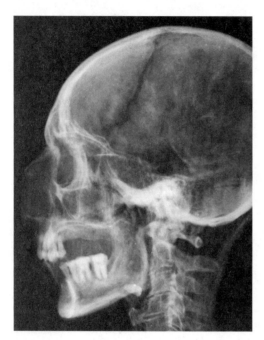

Some scholars believe Merenptah of the Nineteenth Dynasty (about 1210 B.C.) is the pharaoh spoken of in the Bible's book of Exodus, which describes the pharaoh's temporary refusal to let the Hebrew people leave Egypt. This X-ray shows that Merenptah had severe problems with his teeth. Notice that he has no upper teeth at all in the back of his mouth. It is believed that he died around the age of fifty.

One way an Egyptologist can determine the family line of some of the pharaohs is by comparing X-rays of their teeth and facial structures. Since families often have similar features, researchers can compare films of different mummies to decide if they were from the same family. This would confirm when a son followed his father as pharaoh or indicate when the kingdom passed to a different family.

One thing is obvious from the X-rays of the ancient Egyptian pharaohs: most of them had buckteeth. If they were alive today, they would need to visit a good orthodontist to get braces.

But the pharaohs are not the only form of ancient life studied with X-rays. In August 1995, a team of paleontologists led by Dr. Tom Williamson from the New Mexico Museum of Natural History and Science was searching in northwestern New Mexico for dinosaur fossils. One of them, Dr. Robert M. Sullivan from the State Museum of Pennsylvania, saw a bit of bone sticking out of a rock. After the team carefully dug the fossil from its hiding place, they saw it was part of a rare *Parasaurolophus*, one of the dinosaurs shown in the movies *Jurassic Park* and *The Lost World*. Only five other fossils of this type of dinosaur had ever been found before.

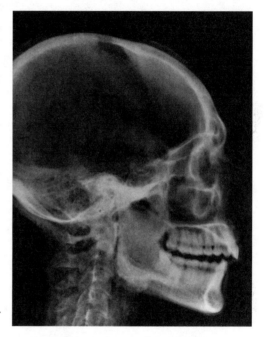

This X-ray shows the skull of Ramses V of the Twentieth Dynasty (about 1150 b.c.). Other than having buckteeth, like most of the pharaohs, he had excellent dental health when he died of smallpox around the age of thirty.

X-rays are the safest way to study the inner secrets of ancient fossils like this one because the rays can see inside them without destroying the fossil by cutting it open. CT scans were taken of the shiny jet-black and dark-brown crest at St. Joseph Medical Center in Albuquerque, New Mexico. Three hundred fifty cross-section CT X-ray images were obtained. Then the images were reconstructed by the computer, allowing the scientists to see the anatomy of the crest. What they showed was a complicated system of three sets of tubes that looped around the inside.

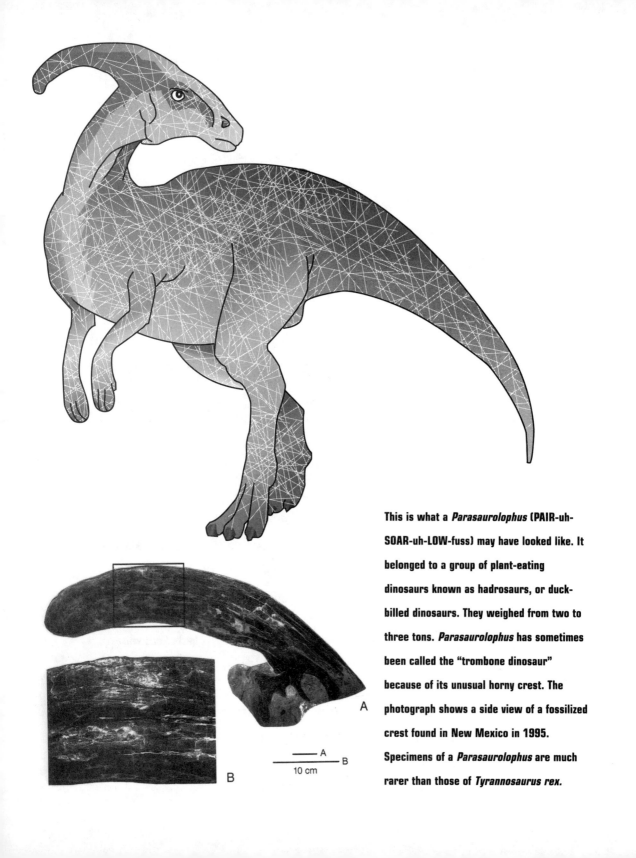

This is what a *Parasaurolophus* (PAIR-uh-SOAR-uh-LOW-fuss) may have looked like. It belonged to a group of plant-eating dinosaurs known as hadrosaurs, or duck-billed dinosaurs. They weighed from two to three tons. *Parasaurolophus* has sometimes been called the "trombone dinosaur" because of its unusual horny crest. The photograph shows a side view of a fossilized crest found in New Mexico in 1995. Specimens of a *Parasaurolophus* are much rarer than those of *Tyrannosaurus rex*.

A

B

A
B
10 cm

The X-ray images confirmed these tubes were connected to the breathing passages of the *Parasaurolophus*.

The specimen this team found is an excellent fossil to study because very few pieces of the skull are missing. The fossilized skull still has the crest sticking out of the back, which gives it the easy-to-recognize look of the *Parasaurolophus*. The crest is not round. At the widest point where it meets the skull bone, it is four inches wide and ten inches deep. It is four and a half feet long, which is about the height of an average ten-year-old.

Paleontologists think the characteristic crest that jutted backward from the animal's head could have helped these dinosaurs recognize each other. Another possible use was suggested by Dr. Tom Williamson and Dr. Carl Diegert of Sandia National Laboratories after studying the CT scans. They believe the *Parasaurolophus* could have used the crest to make sounds that were recognized by others of its kind. The knowledge of the anatomy they learned from the X-ray images helped them study what kind of sound could have been produced by a crest shaped like this one. With this information, they produced a computer-generated sound they believe *Parasaurolophus* might have made when it walked upon the earth. It sounds like a beginning French horn player warming up before the first band concert.

While X-rays are perfect for studying ancient artifacts, they are equally effective in studying more modern artifacts as well. When the RMS *Titanic* sank to the bottom of the North Atlantic on April 15, 1912, no one would have believed that one day the blast of the ship's whistles would be heard again. And X-rays played a part in the effort to toot the massive whistles one last time.

When the *Titanic* set sail, a set of three bronze whistles was mounted on the front smokestack. In 1993, when the whistles were recovered from the bottom of the ocean, they looked much as they did on the night they plunged into the deep, icy sea. Now the whistles are part of a traveling *Titanic* exhibit and are owned by RMS Titanic Inc., the company that salvaged the artifacts. The largest whistle is four feet tall, the midsize one is three feet, and the smallest whistle is one and a half feet.

When they were first recovered, there was no outward sign of harm. However, X-ray studies were needed to see if there was any internal damage that couldn't be seen from the outside. About forty-five X-ray images were taken of the whistles by Braun Intertec. The films showed the whistles were sturdy enough to be blown again.

On February 20, 1999, in St. Paul, Minnesota, a huge crowd gathered to hear the *Titanic*'s whistles for the first time in almost eighty-seven years. The historic sound was digitally recorded to preserve it for the future. The whistles will never be blown again.

Sometimes when articles from the past are studied using modern X-ray methods, ideas that were accepted for many years are proven wrong. This is true in the famous case of Joseph Carey Merrick, who lived in England from 1862 to 1890. Since the time he was a small boy, he was horribly disfigured by a disease that caused huge, smelly masses of lumpy skin that looked like brown cauliflower to grow around his head, body, right hand, and legs. He walked with a cane because of problems with his hips. This was a great misfortune because, throughout his life, this gentle man could never escape from the cruel taunts of people. His looks horrified all who saw him. He made a living for himself in the only way he could—by being on display in a freak show. Merrick became known as the Elephant Man.

Because his skin was rough and darkened like an elephant's, at first many doctors thought Merrick had elephantiasis, a disease that makes body parts swell. Later, many doctors believed he suffered from neurofibromatosis, a disease that causes huge tumors to grow on nerves. Neurofibromatosis is today sometimes called Elephant Man disease.

However, in 1979, at the University of Halifax in Canada, Dr. Michael Cohen, Jr., identified a previously unknown disease, called Proteus syndrome, that causes abnormal growth of bones, skin, and head, as well as other symptoms. Dr. Amita Sharma, a radiologist at the Royal London Hospital, studied Merrick's remains using X-rays and CT scans. These images suggested that the Elephant Man's bones did not demonstrate the symptoms of neurofibromatosis at all. Dr. Sharma believes Merrick suffered from Proteus syndrome, a disease so rare that only an estimated ninety people have ever had it.

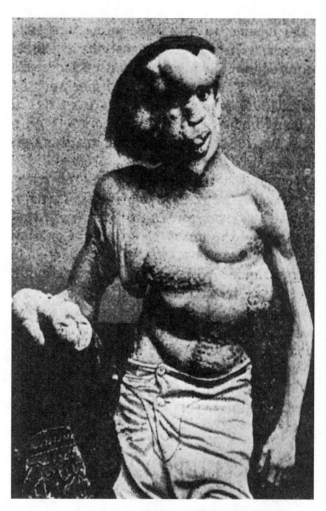

Joseph Carey Merrick, known as the Elephant Man, lived in nineteenth-century England. Today, researchers don't believe he had the disease that became known as the Elephant Man disease.

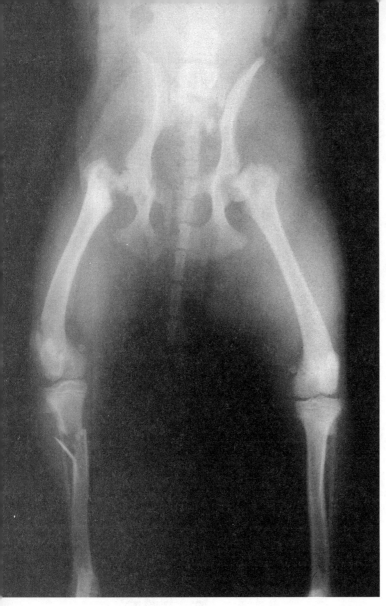

An X-ray of a medium-sized dog who was hit by a car. The film shows the dog's tail between the legs. It also shows serious injuries including breaks in both hips, the femur and tibia on the left side, and at least four places in the pelvis.

Not only can X-rays diagnose disease long after a person's death, they can also help solve the mystery of the identification of an unknown corpse. To do this, X-rays are taken of the body's teeth, then compared with the dental records of missing persons to provide a positive identification. Other body parts that have distinctive characteristics can be used to identify bodies, too. For example, if an X-ray shows a hip or knee replacement, these films can be compared to ones of a missing person to see if they match. Sometimes X-rays can even prove that a murder was committed, by identifying victims and establishing how they were killed.

In a similar way, the National Fish and Wildlife Forensics Laboratory studies dead animals found in the wild. X-rays can show broken bones or bullets that may have been the cause of the animal's death. And, of course, veterinarians use X-rays to diagnose the medical problems of our pets in the same way medical doctors do their human patients.

X-rays are used in another type of scientific study that is out of this world—way out. It is called X-ray astronomy, which is the study of objects in space, such as the sun, stars, and huge star explosions called supernovas, that give off radiation. Since the earth's atmosphere prevents these cosmic X-rays from reaching the earth, the only way to study them is to send an observatory into space.

On July 23, 1999, the National Aeronautics and Space Administration (NASA) launched a new telescope named the Chandra X-ray Observatory to study radiation given off by objects in the universe. This observatory is named in honor of an Indian-American astrophysicist named Subrahmanyan Chandrasekhar, who won a Nobel Prize in 1983 for his study of stars. It is the third of NASA's great earth-orbiting observatories, with others being planned for the future.

The NASA shuttle mission that launched Chandra was the first one commanded by a woman, Colonel Eileen Collins. The Chandra X-ray Observatory is forty-five feet tall and weighs five tons. Its orbit is high above the earth—in fact, it is more than one-third of the way from the earth to the moon.

The polished mirrors on Chandra will focus the radiation emitted by objects in space so that their images can be recorded. The images will be twenty-five times sharper than any photographs obtained before and will allow study of space objects in greater detail. Chandra's focus is so clear it's compared to a person being able to read a newspaper from half a mile away. It is so sensitive that it can observe particles up to the last second before they fall into a black hole.

The Chandra X-ray Observatory as it looks in space. This observatory can collect images of X-rays emitted from deep space by objects that have never been detected before.

In addition to studying black holes, Chandra provides images of objects in the universe that have never been seen before, such as distant exploding stars. These images may be able to tell us more about the size of the universe than we have ever known before.

You've read about how X-rays are used in unusual ways in science, but you have probably personally experienced the most frequent exposure Americans have to X-rays—it's in their dentist's office. About once a year, your dentist or an assistant will take X-rays of your teeth when you go for a routine checkup. They place the tiny film packet inside your mouth and expose the film with a quick X-ray. Then, in the darkroom, they unwrap the film and develop it.

The main thing the dentist is looking for during a checkup is to see if you have any cavities. Cavities are easy to see on X-rays because they look a little darker than healthy teeth do. These dental X-rays show not only the parts of your teeth that you brush each day but also the parts of your teeth that are hidden below your gum line. X-rays will show if there is an infection, called an abscess, around the roots of a tooth. They also show teeth that you wouldn't otherwise know you had, the ones that are forming in your gums but have not pushed through yet.

Sometimes your dentist may want to take an X-ray of all of your teeth on the same film instead of a lot of little films. This is a panoramic view, sometimes called a panograph. The finished X-ray film looks as if your jaw has been straightened out flat instead of curving. Panographs are made with a special machine that takes pictures as it rotates around your head. With this kind of X-ray, your dentist can see how your whole jaw and all your teeth look, and see if there are any problems with the bones that surround your teeth, if you have any missing teeth, or if your teeth are coming in crooked.

For more than one hundred years the basic way to take and keep dental and medical X-rays has been the same: a piece of film is exposed by X-rays to produce an image, the film is developed with chemicals, and the finished product is an X-ray film. After the doctor looks at it by hanging it on a lighted view box, it is put in a folder and kept for further reference.

However, in the future there may not be any more X-ray films that you hold in your hand and keep in a file. Technology is now available that will do away with physical films completely.

The new system is called the Picture Archives and Communication System (PACS). It will allow an X-ray to be taken in the usual way, then digitally record the image on magnetic tape, instead of on a traditional X-ray film. All of the records will be copied in another location to ensure the safety of the images. When doctors want to see a patient's X-ray, they

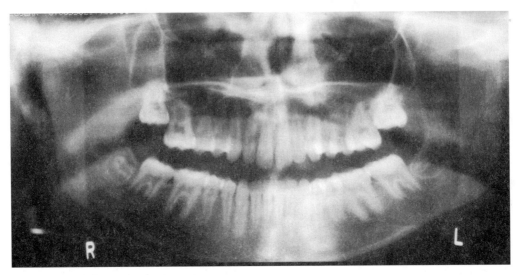

This panoramic view shows all the teeth of a twelve-year-old girl. She has no cavities. At each end of the teeth on the bottom, you can see where her wisdom teeth are forming.

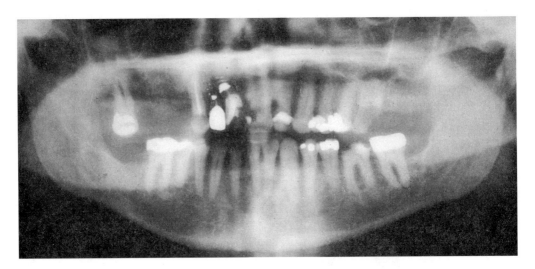

This is a panoramic view of the teeth of a man in his fifties. He has cavities (dark spots) that have eroded away large parts of several teeth. He also has several missing teeth. Fillings (bright white areas) can be seen in most of the teeth he has left. There is evidence of previous root canal procedures in two of his upper teeth, one of which has a crown. A film like this sort of makes you want to go brush and floss, doesn't it?

can go to a special computer and monitor that is designed for the system and choose their patient's X-ray file. The doctors will look at the X-rays on a computer monitor instead of on a view box. There will not be a film that you can hold in your hand, although the system is capable of printing out the image on paper if needed.

There are several advantages to this system. With the old way, X-ray films are thrown away after a few years because of limited space for storage. With the new system, the X-ray images can be kept forever, because they are stored on tape. Another advantage to PACS is that the image can be enlarged, darkened, or lightened to allow the doctor to see a questionable area better. Also, these images can be sent to another PACS anywhere in the world in a matter of seconds. For example, this will be helpful if a patient is in a rural area where a specialist may be needed to read the X-ray. The image can be sent quickly to a larger medical center where a radiologist can read it and give the diagnosis right away.

X-rays have become an indispensable tool in scientific research. Objects can be studied with X-rays that would have been impossible without them. With them, it is possible not only to examine your teeth but to examine the teeth of a pharaoh who ruled the shifting sands of Egypt thousands of years ago. X-rays can explore the secrets of the dinosaurs, as well as the secrets of distant galaxies—and almost everything in between.

9 THE INDUSTRIOUS X-RAY

Not only have X-rays been important in the scientific world, they have also been used in industry since the early days of their discovery. Two films taken by Dr. Roentgen when he tested X-rays inspired many uses in business and industry.

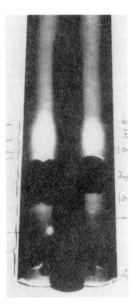

First, Dr. Roentgen's film of his shotgun clearly showed the interior of the shotgun—and even demonstrated a flaw. This image proved X-rays could see inside machinery as well as the human body.

When the war departments of the United States, Germany, and Austria saw the gun's image, they immediately realized the possibility of testing the

Can you see the lead pellets in this X-ray of Dr. Roentgen's own double-barreled shotgun? He wrote notes on the image about the shells, markings, and a defect he saw in the gun's barrel. It is officially marked W. C. Röntgen, Würzburg, in the lower right corner.

quality of weapons with X-rays. It is ironic that, during times of war, X-rays were used to make sure guns would work correctly on the battlefield. Then, when they did work and caused injuries to the enemy, X-rays were used to diagnose the damage done by those guns.

This British soldier is getting an X-ray of his injured left shoulder during the Sudanese wars (1896–98). The equipment is outdoors because of the sweltering heat along the Nile River. Notice that the X-ray tube is connected to a series of batteries.

The second of Dr. Roentgen's images that had a far-reaching effect was a film of zinc strips welded together. The image didn't look like much, but it showed minute variations in the thickness of the metal that could not be seen by the naked eye. This inspired the use of X-rays to examine metal to detect otherwise hidden flaws.

The ability of X-rays to see through metal has been used in industry in countless ways. Today, large pieces of metal equipment, such as airplane wings, are inspected with X-rays to look for defects. Films will show if there are any weak spots or gas holes in the metal sheets or in the welds that hold big pieces together.

NASA uses X-rays, too. Parts of the space shuttle, including the welds in the solid rocket boosters, are inspected with X-rays. They can also be used to see if there are any loose screws (in the equipment, not the crew) before liftoff.

Not only are X-rays used to see through metal, they are used to see through all sorts of other objects, too. X-rays are used in building electronics equipment by finding the exact position to drill holes in the circuit board. They are even used in sawmills. Thick logs are X-rayed to detect knots, rot, or other defects. If the film reveals a flaw, the sawmill chooses the best way to cut the log to produce the best boards with the least amount of waste. X-rays are even used to make sure there are no bones in the chicken nuggets you might eat for lunch.

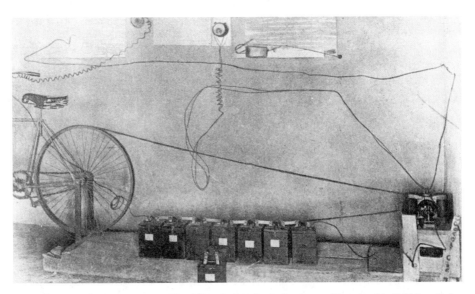

Conditions were primitive in the Nile Valley during the Sudanese conflicts. At this field hospital, the batteries that ran the X-ray tube were charged with the help of a stationary bicycle. Soldiers took turns pedaling the bicycle to generate electricity.

Some industries use X-rays to study individual elements in a product. This process, called X-ray powder diffraction, became possible as a result of the work of Max von Laue in Munich, Germany, in 1912. In his research, he made X-ray films of crystals which proved that the atoms that make up different elements are arranged in unique patterns. Today, this method is used to make sure there are no impurities and the chemical makeup is correct in such products as glass, paint pigments, soaps, soil, medications, and wooden utility poles.

Industries use X-rays in various ways to ensure the public safety. This is ironic considering the fact that X-rays can be a danger to public safety if not used correctly. In the 1940s, researchers decided a universal symbol was needed to warn people about areas that use radiation. Various colors and symbols that might be used were discussed. One suggestion was to use the skull and crossbones, like a pirate flag. Another was a mushroom cloud, which is the shape of the cloud an atomic bomb makes when it explodes.

At last the symbol was agreed upon. It is a magenta, or sometimes black, symbol on a bright yellow background. The dark parts look like the three blades of a fan, each having a 60-degree arc. It is now used as the international symbol for radiation danger throughout the world and is posted anywhere radiation could be in use.

The international symbol for radiation danger, usually posted on every X-ray room door and any other areas that may be using radiation.

One place where X-rays are used for the public safety is in airports. In the 1970s, when airplanes were being hijacked at an alarming rate, airport security began using X-rays to look inside the carry-on luggage of travelers before they boarded planes. The fluoroscope machine would reveal any weapon such as a gun, knife, or bomb that might be hidden in a bag. This safety measure is still used today. Even luggage that will ride in the cargo area of the plane is often checked by X-rays.

Another way X-rays assist the public safety is by their use in law enforcement. When a suspicious package is found that could be a bomb, the bomb squad is called in. Getting an X-ray of the package is their first line of defense. While the officers are at a safe distance of about twenty-five feet, a special, portable, remote-controlled machine takes an X-ray film of the package. This film shows the bomb squad if the contents contain explosives.

The food industry has begun to irradiate food to make it safer and cleaner, and to prolong its shelf life. To accomplish this, various foods are exposed to X-rays or other forms of radiation to kill salmonella, *E. coli*, and other bacteria. Millions of Americans get sick and nine thousand die each year from food poisoning. Radiation could reduce these statistics.

Studies done by the Food and Drug Administration (FDA) have shown that irradiating food reduces or eliminates bacteria, parasites, and insects found in food products. The FDA has approved food irradiation for treating meat, poultry, dry spices, seasonings, fresh fruits, and vegetables, and has established guidelines for how much radiation each food can receive.

Irradiating food does not sterilize the food, but it does destroy most of the harmful bacteria. After food has been irradiated, just as when food is processed in any way, such as by freezing, canning, or cooking, changes occur that result in new harmless substances being present that were not there before. Studies by the FDA found there was no danger in eating these substances.

Some people are against the use of food irradiation for different reasons: fear that safety practices at processing plants will be relaxed, or that irradiation will reduce nutrients in food. Some don't want an irradiation facility near their homes, while others are fearful of radiation and suspect irradiated food may be harmful. Supporters point out that irradiated food is not radioactive, just as your teeth are not radioactive after they have been X-rayed by the dentist. Important organizations have approved the use of food irradiation, such as the World Health Organization, the American Medical Association, and the United States Department of Agriculture. The fear of food irradiation could be compared to the fears the public had about safety when pasteurized milk and the microwave oven were new ideas. When the public understood the safety of these products, they became staples in many people's lives.

Although the idea of food irradiation is new to the grocery store, astronauts have been eating irradiated food for years. The cost of irradiated food in stores will be higher than non-irradiated products because of the additional processing step, but safer and longer-lasting products may be worth the extra price. Irradiated strawberries will stay fresh for up to three weeks, compared to three to five days for non-irradiated strawberries. Eventually, the public will determine the success or failure of food irradiation when they shop at the supermarket.

So that the public will know what they are buying, all irradiated food sold in a grocery store must be marked with the radura symbol.

Other things besides food can be irradiated to make products safer. Medical supplies such as needles, gloves, gowns, syringes, sutures, and bandages are sterilized using radiation. Cosmetics companies also use irradiation to kill microorganisms in their raw materials that might contaminate their products. Finished products such as applicators, bottles, brushes, lotions, and shampoos are irradiated to kill bacteria.

The international symbol for food irradiation, called the radura. It is to be printed with green ink. The petals represent food, and the five breaks in the circle represent rays from the radiation source. According to the Food and Drug Administration, this symbol must appear on any food product that has been irradiated, along with the words "Treated by irradiation" or "Treated with radiation."

It seems that almost every industry has found a way to use X-rays. Some companies use them to find hidden flaws in their products; others use them to protect the safety of the public. So the next time you board an airplane, think about how many ways X-rays could have been used: in manufacturing the wings; in checking your luggage for security reasons; to prolong the shelf life of parts of your in-flight meal; or to test the chemical makeup of the soap in the washroom or the paint that covers the plane.

10 WHAT'S NEXT?

X-rays have become so much a part of our world, it makes you wonder how earlier generations lived without them. As we've learned, the mysterious rays have influenced everything from art, music, science, industry, television, advertising, and comic books to law enforcement.

What we know about X-rays and how they are used often seems contradictory. X-rays can hurt people but they help people, too. X-rays can cause cancer but they can also treat cancer. X-rays were used for beauty treatments but they also caused disfiguring scars. At first X-rays were mesmerizing and displayed like a sideshow exhibit, but now they are so familiar we often don't give them a second glance. X-rays have caused hundreds of deaths, but today they are used to keep the public safe. X-rays can be used to study tiny atoms in a crystal, as well as huge objects like stars. All these things are true—the X-ray is a paradox.

In spite of the many high-tech ways X-rays are used today, still the greatest impact of the discovery of X-rays remains the ability to "see" inside the human body. As soon as the first ghostly image of Bertha Roentgen's hand was cabled around the world, medical practice was changed for-ever.

And from the earliest films the race was on to make X-ray images better and faster. Each improvement in equipment and film through the years paved the way for the next improvement. As a result, X-rays of the body that once took over an hour of exposure now take only a fraction of one second. As equipment improved, diagnostic tests became possible that had once been impossible. Today, X-rays are used to take pictures of every part of the human body. Yet progress continues as ever better equipment and methods of medical imaging are developed.

Wilhelm Conrad Roentgen could not have imagined the incredible ways his discovery would be used. He had no idea the weird, wacky, and wonderful X-ray would come to hold such an important place in the every-day lives of people.

X-rays have come so far in the first hundred years it makes you wonder how they might be used in the next hundred years.

Just imagine . . .

GLOSSARY

ABSCESS An infection characterized by inflamed tissue, often around the root of a tooth.

ALUMINUM A silver-white metal that is both lightweight and strong. X-rays can pass through aluminum easily.

ARMAMENTARIUM All the equipment and resources in a doctor's office.

ARTHRITIS A disease that causes the body's joints to swell and become painful.

ASTROPHYSICIST An astronomer who studies the physical properties and behavior of the universe.

CATHODE RAYS Invisible rays that are emitted from the cathode (negative electrical connection) of a Crookes tube when high-voltage electricity passes through it.

CLUBFOOT A deformity of the foot that is present at birth.

COLOR BLINDNESS An inherited visual defect that causes an inability to perceive differences between certain colors, such as red and green.

CREST A tuft or projecting part extending from the head of an animal. In the case of the *Parasaurolophus*, it is the hornlike object protruding from the top of its head.

CROOKES TUBE A glass vacuum tube developed by William Crookes in the 1870s that had both a positive and a negative electrical connection. At the time of the discovery of X-rays, every physical science laboratory had a Crookes tube as part of its basic equipment.

CT SCAN A sophisticated X-ray machine that takes many images of an object one small section at a time. "CT" is an abbreviation for "computed tomography." A CT scan is also sometimes called a CAT scan.

ELECTROMAGNETIC RADIATION Energy that travels in varying wavelengths, such as light, radio waves, and X-rays.

ELECTRONS Negatively charged particles that surround the nucleus of an atom.

ELEPHANTIASIS A disease that causes the skin of the affected body parts to become enlarged, rough, and thickened.

ERYTHEMA DOSE A measurement of radiation used in the early days of X-rays. This dose was determined by the length of time it took for a person's skin to turn red after being exposed to X-rays.

FLUORESCENT Having the ability, found in certain substances, to give off light when exposed to radiation.

FLUOROSCOPE An X-ray machine that allows the user to see an image on a fluorescent screen while X-rays are being produced, without creating a permanent image.

FOSSIL Hardened remains in rocks of animals or plants that lived long ago, or traces of them that were impressed into mud or sand that has since hardened into rock.

INDUCTION COIL A device that takes a low-voltage electric current and transforms it through a looped wire into a higher-voltage electric current.

NEUROFIBROMATOSIS A disease, sometimes called Elephant Man disease, that affects the nervous system and skin, causing brown spots and tumors to grow.

NOBEL PRIZE An important international prize awarded each year for outstanding work in six different categories: physics, chemistry, medicine, literature, economics, and peace. The first prizes were given in 1901.

OBSERVATORY A place where heavenly bodies are studied. X-ray observatories are built specifically to analyze radiation given off by objects in the universe.

PALEONTOLOGIST A scientist who studies prehistoric life by means of fossil remains.

PARASAUROLOPHUS (PAIR-uh-SOAR-uh-LOW-fuss) A plant-eating, duck-billed dinosaur.

PATHOLOGIST A medical doctor who studies the cause and nature of diseases.

PLATINUM A silver-colored metal. X-rays do not pass through platinum easily.

POLIO (Poliomyelitis) A disease causing inflammation of the brain and spinal cord that sometimes causes paralysis.

PROTEUS SYNDROME A rare disease that causes abnormal growth of the bones, skin, and head.

RADIOLOGIST A medical doctor who specializes in reading X-rays.

RINGWORM A contagious skin disease caused by a fungus.

ROENTGEN International unit used to measure radiation, for example, from X-rays.

SCOLIOSIS An abnormal condition of the spine where the vertebrae curve to the side.

SUPERNOVA A very large star that explodes, suddenly becoming very bright, then gradually fading.

TUBERCULOSIS (TB) An infectious disease that causes lumps in the body, most often in the lungs.

ULCERATION A festering open sore.

VACUUM A space from which all or nearly all the air has been taken out.

VACUUM TUBE Any sealed glass tube, including a Crookes tube, from which most of the air has been removed, and which contains both a positive and negative electrical connection.

VIVISECTION Medical experiments, especially surgery, on live animals for the purpose of research.

VOLT A unit of measurement of the force of an electric current.

VOLTAGE Movement of electricity that is measured in volts.

WAVELENGTH The distance between a point of a wave of electromagnetic radiation to the identical point in the next wave.

X-RAY ASTRONOMY The study of objects in space, such as stars and supernovas, by observing the X-ray radiation they give off.

X-RAY POWDER DIFFRACTION A method of using X-rays to study the pattern of atoms in different elements.

X-RAYS Invisible rays of electromagnetic radiation that have a very short wavelength. X-rays have the ability to penetrate some objects.

ZINC A bluish-white metal. X-rays do not pass through zinc easily.

SELECTED BIBLIOGRAPHY

The research material for this book came from sources too numerous to list here, including books; medical, art, and photography journals; periodicals; newspapers; consumer reports; Web sites; and personal communications with the author. The following is a selected list of significant works consulted.

Arnau, Frank. *The Art of the Faker: Three Thousand Years of Deception*. Trans. J. Maxwell Brownjohn. Boston: Little, Brown, 1961.

Brecher, Ruth and Edward. *The Rays: A History of Radiology in the United States and Canada*. Baltimore: Williams and Walkins Co., 1969.

Brown, Percy, M.D. *American Martyrs to Science through the Roentgen Rays*. Springfield, Ill.: Charles C. Thomas, 1936.

Bruwer, André J., ed. *Classic Descriptions in Diagnostic Roentgenology*. 2 vols. Springfield, Ill.: Charles C. Thomas, 1964.

Caufield, Catherine. *Multiple Exposures: Chronicles of the Radiation Age*. New York: Harper and Row, 1989.

del Regato, Juan A., M.D. *Radiological Physicists*. New York: American Association of Physicists in Medicine, 1985.

Dewing, Stephen B., M.D. *Modern Radiology in Historical Perspective*. Springfield, Ill.: Charles
C. Thomas, 1962.

Eisenberg, Ronald L., M.D. *Radiology: An Illustrated History*. St. Louis: Mosby Year Book,
1992.

Etter, Lewis E., ed. *The Science of Ionizing Radiation*. Springfield, Ill.: Charles C. Thomas,
1965.

Glasser, Otto. *Dr. W. C. Roentgen*. Springfield, Ill.: Charles C. Thomas, 1945.

———. *Wilhelm Conrad Röntgen and the Early History of the Roentgen Rays*. Springfield, Ill.:
Charles C. Thomas, 1934. Translation.

Grey, Vivian. *Roentgen's Revolution*. Boston: Little, Brown, 1973.

Harris, James E., and Kent R. Weeks. *X-raying the Pharaohs*. New York: Scribner, 1973.

———, eds. *An X Ray Atlas of the Royal Mummies*. Chicago: University of Chicago Press,
1980.

Jones, Mark, ed. *Fake? The Art of Deception*. Berkeley and Los Angeles: Trustees of the British
Museum, 1990.

Kassabian, Mihran Krikor, M.D. *Röntgen Rays and Electro-Therapeutics*. 2nd ed. Philadelphia:
J. B. Lippincott, 1910.

Mould, Richard F. *A Century of X Rays and Radioactivity in Medicine: With Emphasis on Photographic Records of the Early Years*. Bristol and Philadelphia: Institute of Physics Publish-
ing, 1993.

Nitske, W. Robert. *The Life of Wilhelm Conrad Röntgen, Discoverer of the X Ray*. Tucson: University of Arizona Press, 1971.

Schubert, Jack, and Ralph E. Lapp. *Radiation: What It Is and How It Affects You*. New York:
Viking, 1957.

Selman, Joseph, M.D. *The Fundamentals of X-ray and Radium Physics*, 5th ed. Springfield, Ill.:
Charles C. Thomas, 1976.

Sullivan, Robert M., and Thomas E. Williamson. *A New Skull of Parasaurolophus (Dinosauria:
Hadrosauridae) from the Kirtland Formation of New Mexico and a Revision of the Genus*. Al-
buquerque: U.S. Bureau of Land Management and the State Museum of Pennsylvania,
Pennsylvania Historical and Museum Commission, Harrisburg, 1999.

RECOMMENDED FURTHER READING

Adams, Simon. *Titanic.* New York: Dorling Kindersley, 1999.

This book shows the RMS *Titanic* from the shipyard to the graveyard. It is illustrated with historical photographs, underwater images of the ship, and photographs of victims' personal effects and artifacts recovered from the ocean floor.

Burroughs, Alan. *Art Criticism from a Laboratory.* Westport, Conn.: Greenwood Press, 1965.

Famous paintings are discussed and analyzed using X-rays.

Daniels, Les. *Marvel: Five Fabulous Decades of the World's Greatest Comics.* New York: Abrams, 1991.

Filled with full-color photographs, this book will entertain even those who aren't comic-book readers. It gives facts about the history behind comic-book characters as well as information about their creators. Although Marvel comic books are the focus of the book, recognition is given to Superman, a DC Comics character, for being the original example that all future superheroes would follow.

Haines, Tim. *Walking with Dinosaurs.* New York: Dorling Kindersley, 2000.

   The pictures in this book make you think you have stumbled into a land where dinosaurs go about their daily lives. The lifelike illustrations were created with simulated nature photography and computer graphics. A skull of a *Parasaurolophus* is shown and its crest briefly discussed.

Harris, James E., and Kent R. Weeks. *X-raying the Pharaohs.* New York: Scribner's, 1973.

   Instead of pyramids and secret tombs, the Egyptian Museum in Cairo is now the resting place for Egyptian pharaohs. This book details the study of their mummies using X-rays. It contains photographs, X-ray images, and information about these ancient rulers.

Rachlin, Harvey. *Lucy's Bones, Sacred Stones, and Einstein's Brain.* New York: Henry Holt, 1996.

   Brief accounts of objects from the pages of history are pictured and described, and their present-day locations are given. Many objects are detailed, including the Elephant Man's bones, George Washington's false teeth, the Gettysburg Address, London Bridge, and Anne Frank's diary.

Thomson, Peggy, and Barbara Moore. *The Nine-Ton Cat: Behind the Scenes at an Art Museum.* Boston: Houghton Mifflin, 1997.

   This book gives a behind-the-scenes peek into the National Gallery of Art in Washington, D.C. It details the conservation story, including an X-ray exam, of the only painting in America by Leonardo da Vinci. Also, an X-ray of a wax sculpture by Edgar Degas is pictured that reveals not only repair work previously done but also the presence of a salt-shaker lid embedded in the piece.

WEB SITES

http://www.nmmnh-abq.mus.nm.us/nmmnh/soundsandimages.html

You can hear for yourself the computer-generated sound the *Parasaurolophus* may have made and learn how the sound was produced. This site provides links to learn more about the *Parasaurolophus*.

http://www.titanic-online.com/events/index.htm

The digitally recorded sound of the *Titanic*'s whistles that were blown in St. Paul, Minnesota, can be accessed here. Another section lists the names of the passengers and indicates who perished and who survived. Other links leads you to more information about *Titanic*, including photographs of the ship being built, the expedition to locate *Titanic*, artifacts from the sunken ship, and more.

http://www.jsitton.pwp.blueyonder.co.uk/elephant_man.htm

This Web site contains information about Joseph Merrick, known as the Elephant Man. A letter written by Merrick and his autobiography are displayed on this site. Information about Merrick's medical treatment taken from the writings of his doctor, Dr. Treves, is given here, along with a link to learn more about the Proteus Foundation.

http://www.thursdaysclassroom.com

This site links NASA's latest research to the classroom. Students will enjoy the fascinating information found there. Teachers will be delighted to find fully developed lesson plans ready to use in the classroom.

http://chandra.nasa.gov/chandra.html

This NASA Chandra X-ray Observatory news page contains the latest Chandra images from space and links you to other Chandra information.

ACKNOWLEDGMENTS

I'd like to thank my husband, Pat, for his love and support through the years it has taken for this book to become a reality. I would also like to thank my editor, Robbie Mayes, for his excellent editorial advice and for sharing a vision of what this book could be. The American College of Radiology and Jim Morrison were generous in allowing me to use many of the historical photographs reproduced in these pages. I'm especially grateful to my friend Dr. Max L. Baker, professor of radiology at the University of Arkansas for Medical Sciences, who has helped me in invaluable ways. I'd also like to thank the Society of Children's Book Writers and Illustrators for their confidence in this book by awarding me the 1997 Work-in-Progress Grant.

A project like this is not possible without the input of many people who have answered countless questions and generously shared their time, knowledge, films, and more with me. The following have my deepest appreciation: Arkansas Children's Hospital; Arkansas Hand Center; Recep Avci; Ann Baty; Dr. Lance Bogoslavsky; Tom Bousque; Ann Brogley; Donna Chapman; Collector's Edition Comics in North Little Rock, Arkansas; Dr. Carl Digert; Food Technology Service, Inc.; Dr. Paul Frame; Ken Goddard; Lethlyn Harp; James E. Harris; Captain William F. Holcomb; Susan and Brenna House; Nancy Jackson; Kate Judge; Erick Kalenberg; Stan Katz; Dr. Reed Kilgore; Dr. Sally Klein; Bob McCoy; Brooks McKinney; Ed

ACKNOWLEDGMENTS

....

Nicholson; Dionne and Kylie Patterson; Pluritec Information Department; Joe Reeves; Dr. Peter Ritchie; Susan Rose; Mada Ritter; Dr. Steve Sirr; Jennifer Snyder; SteriGenics; Karen Tucker; Manuel Uhm; Larry White; Tommy Wilder; and Dr. Thomas Williamson. And last but not least, Darcy Pattison and my writers' group.

Carla Killough McClafferty

ILLUSTRATION CREDITS

Artwork and permission to reprint many of the images in this book have been generously provided by the American College of Radiology. These pictures appear on the following pages: 6 (top and bottom), 13, 21, 25, 26 (top and bottom), 27, 28, 29, 30, 35, 37, 39, 41, 44 (top and bottom), 53, 54, 63, 64, 67, 68, 69, 73, 75, 94, and 112. The frontispiece and the X-ray of the catcher's mitt on the title page are courtesy of the author. The other two title-page images are courtesy of Dr. Max L. Baker.

The remainder are credited as follows:

Page 7   Deutsches Museum

12   Deutsches Röntgen Museum

14   Source: Ronald L. Eisenberg, M.D., *Radiology: An Illustrated History*

15   Rendered by Tim Hall

16   *St. Louis Post-Dispatch*

18   Deutsches Röntgen Museum

23   (top and bottom) *Life* magazine, 1896

38   Eisenberg, *Radiology*

42   (top and bottom) Eisenberg, *Radiology*

43   (left and right) Eisenberg, *Radiology*

47   Eisenberg, *Radiology*

50   (all pictures) Courtesy of the author

56   (top and bottom) Eisenberg, *Radiology*

71   Eisenberg, *Radiology*

82   Courtesy Bob McCoy, Museum of Questionable Medical Practices,
        Minneapolis, Minnesota

87   (top and bottom) Metropolitan Museum of Art

88   (top and bottom) Metropolitan Museum of Art

89   (left and right) Virginia Museum of Fine Arts

90   Wow Them, Inc., P.O. Box 940432, Far Rockaway, NY, 11694;
        e-mail: WowThemInc@aol.com

91   (all pictures) Courtesy Dr. Steven Sirr

92   DC Comics. Superman is a trademark of DC Comics © 2001. All rights
        reserved. Used with permission

93   Eisenberg, *Radiology*

96   (left and right) Courtesy Dr. James E. Harris

97   (left and right) Courtesy Dr. James E. Harris

98   Courtesy Dr. James E. Harris

99   Courtesy Dr. James E. Harris

100   (top) Rendered by Tim Hall

100   (bottom) New Mexico Museum of Natural History and Science

103   London Hospital

104   (top and bottom) Courtesy Dr. Lance Bogoslavsky

106   NASA

108   (top and bottom) Courtesy Dr. Peter Richie

110   Deutsches Museum

111   Eisenberg, *Radiology*

113   Rendered by Tim Hall

116   Rendered by Tim Hall

INDEX

acne, treatment of, 43

Agriculture, U.S. Department of, 115

aluminum, 8, 11, 12

American Medical Association, 73, 115

American Technical Book Company, 31

American X-Ray Journal, The, 40, 41

Army, U.S., 66

art, 85–88

Art Journal, 85

asthma, treatment of, 43

astronomy, X-ray, 105–6, 121

Baetjer, Frederick, 65

Bearded Man with a Velvet Cap (Flinck), 88

Béclère, Antoine, 75–76

Bible, the, 98

birthmarks, removal of, 42

bones, development of, 51

Boveri, Theodor, 9

brain, X-rays of, 27–28

British Journal of Photography, The, 36, 45, 49–51, 56

Buckwalter, H. H., 46, 47

calcium tungstate, 28

cancer, 42, 68–71, 73

cartilage, 51

cartoons of X-rays, 22–23

cathode rays, 7, 8, 10, 119

Chandrasekhar, Subrahmanyan, 105

Chandra X-ray Observatory, 105–6

Cole, Lewis Gregory, 38, 40

Collins, Colonel Eileen, 105

Columbia University, 34, 58, 78, 79

computed tomography (CT), 89–91, 99, 103, 119–20

cosmetics industry, uses of X-rays in, 115

Crookes, William, 5, 119

Crookes tubes, 5, 7, 8, 12, 119

cubists, 85

Dally, Clarence, 63–65, 81

Daniel, John, 55

deaths, radiation as cause of, 26, 63–69, 74–76

Degas, Edgar, 89

demonstrations of X-rays, 17, 29–30

dental X-rays, 37, 38, 106–8

depression, treatment of, 43

Diegert, Carl, 101

dinosaurs, 99–101

dosimeter, 69

Dudley, William, 55

eczema, treatment of, 43

Eder, J. M., 41

Edison, Thomas, 26–30, 63, 64, 78, 81

Electrical Engineer, The, 27, 59, 62

Electrical Review, 61, 80

Electrical World, 26, 62

Electrician, The, 24–25

Electric Light Association Exposition, 28–31

electromagnetic radiation, 14–15, 120

elephantiasis, 102–3, 120

Elephant Man (Joseph Carey Merrick), 102–3

epiphyses, 51

equipment testing by X-ray, 111

erythema dose, 54, 120

Falk, Hilbert L., 27

fear of X-rays, 13, 24, 30, 34

Ffolliott, Gladys, 45

"film badge" (dosimeter), 69

Fleischmann, Elizabeth, 65–67

Flinck, Govert, 88

fluoroscopes, 28–30, 52–55, 63, 69, 70, 80–83, 120

Food and Drug Administration (FDA), 114

food irradiation, 114–15

forgeries, detection of, 85–86

Frankfurter Zeitung, 32

Freund, Leopold, 40–44

Fuchs, Wolfram, 26

gallstones, detection of, 26

General Electric Laboratory, 62

Geyser, Albert C., 70, 72

Glasser, Otto, 46

Grant, W. W., 46, 47

hair loss, X-rays as cause of, 40, 55–56, 64

hair removal, 41–42, 56–57, 72–74

Halifax, University of, 103

Hascheck, E., 37

Hawks, Herbert, 58–60

Herman Doomer (Rembrandt), 87

Horse at Trough (Degas), 89

induction coil, 26, 120

industry, uses of X-rays in, 110–16

injuries, radiation as cause of, 11, 40, 44, 53–55, 57–74

International Congress of Radiology, 74

Johns Hopkins Hospital, 65

Johnson, George, 79

Jones, Fred, 60

Journal of the American Medical Association, The, 73

Kassabian, Mihran, 33, 34, 69–71
kidney stones, detection of, 39
Kölliker, Albert von, 17
König, Walter, 37

Lacombe, Colonel C. F., 45, 46
Lancet, The, 55
Laue, Max von, 112–13
law enforcement, uses of X-rays in, 114
lead, blocking of X-rays by, 8, 12, 68
LeFevre, Owen, 46–47
legal cases, X-rays and, 45–51, 69
Levy, William, 60–61
Life magazine, 80
light, visible, 14, 15
Lindenthal, O. T., 37
Lindsey, Ben B., 47–48
Literary Digest, 45
London Hospital, 44
London Standard, 16, 79

Macuse, Dr., 57
Mandel, John, 78
Marconi, Guglielmo, 3
McKinley, William, 81
medicine, uses of X-rays in, 26, 32–44
Merrick, Joseph Carey (the Elephant Man), 102–3
microwaves, 14
Minnesota, University of, 60–61
Morton, William J., 31, 53, 78

Mountain Electric Company, 45
mummies, Egyptian, 95–99
Münchener Medizinische Wochenschrift, 58

National Aeronautics and Space Administration (NASA), 105, 111
National Fish and Wildlife Forensics Laboratory, 104
neurofibromatosis, 103
New England Journal of Medicine, 83
New Mexico Museum of Natural History and Science, 99
New York Times, The, 20–21, 27, 31, 77
Nobel Prize, 18, 105, 120

"On a New Kind of Ray" (Roentgen), 14
Orme, George, 49

patents, refused by Roentgen, 21
Photography, 22
photography of X-rays, 10–12, 34
Picture Archives and Communication System (PACS), 107, 109
Pitkin, John, 65
Poech, R., 36
portraits, 31
Punzo, James, 49
Pupin, Michael, 34

radar waves, 14
radiation danger, international symbol for, 113
radiation sickness, 65
radiation therapy, 41–42

radiographers, 54–55

radio waves, 14

radura symbol, 115, 116

Ramses V, Pharaoh of Egypt, 99

Rembrandt, 87, 88

ringworm, treatment of, 43, 44

Robarts, Herbert, 40

roentgen (unit of radiation), 74

Roentgen, Bertha, 13, 14, 16, 19, 32, 117–18

Roentgen, Wilhelm Conrad, 5–21, 27, 110,
    111, 118

Rogers, Ingles, 78

Röntgen Rays and Electro-Therapeutics
    (Kassabian), 33

Royal London Hospital, 103

St. Georg Hospital monument, Hamburg,
    Germany, 74–76

St. Louis Post-Dispatch, 16

Sandia National Laboratories, 101

Scientific American, 48–49

security, uses of X-rays in, 80–81, 113–14

Sharma, Amita, 103

shoes, use of X-rays in fitting, 82–83

Sirr, Steven, 90

skin problems, treatment of, 42–43

Slater, Henry, 79

Smith, James, 46–48

soft-tissue X-ray images, 37–39

Spanish-American War, 66, 69

State Museum of Pennsylvania, 99

Stradivari, Antonio, 91

studios, X-ray, 26

Sudanese wars, 111, 112

Sullivan, Robert M., 99

Superman, 92–93

Thomson, Elihu, 62, 63

Titanic, RMS, 101–2

tuberculosis, use of X-rays in diagnosis of,
    40

Vanderbilt University, 55

veins, X-rays of, 37–39

Vienna, University of, 41

Vienna Presse, 15

violin, X-ray of, 91

visible light, 14, 15

Wagner, Rome, 67–69

Wagner, Thurman, 67–69

Wasson, Walter, 45–46

wave length, of electromagnetic radiation,
    14–15

weapons testing by X-ray, 111

whooping cough, treatment of, 43

Wilhelm II, Emperor of Germany, 18

Willard, Frances E., 80

Williams, Francis H., 25

Williamson, Tom, 99, 101

Women's Christian Temperance Union, 80

World Health Organization, 115

World War II, 18

Würzburg, University of, 5, 10

X-ray powder diffraction, 112

zinc, blocking of X-rays by, 11, 12, 121